# BATTLE RATTLE
## A LAST MEMOIR OF WORLD WAR II

# BATTLE RATTLE

## A LAST MEMOIR OF WORLD WAR II

## ROGER BOAS

**STINSON PUBLISHING**
San Francisco

Published by
Stinson Publishing
San Francisco, California
www.battlerattlememoir.com

All photos are from the author's personal collection or donated by friends.

Cover and book design by Nicole Hayward

LIBRARY OF CONGRESS CONTROL NUMBER: 2015915241

First Edition

ISBN: 978-0-9967567-0-9 (paperback)
ISBN: 978-0-9967567-2-3 (hardcover)
ISBN: 978-0-9967567-1-6 (ebook)

Printed in the United States of America

There were 10,000 men in the Fourth Armored Division when we went overseas to England in December 1943. Only 8,500 of us returned.

This book is dedicated to the 1,500 men who gave their lives to stop the horrific Nazi menace, including my fellow forward observers John Kelly, Dude Dent, and Bill Sovacool.

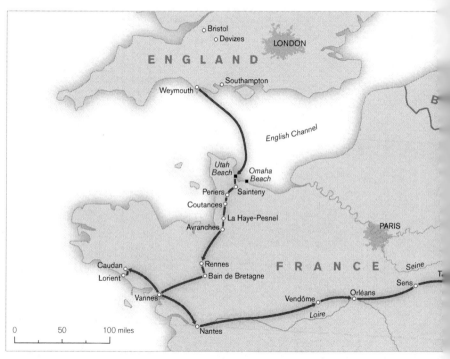

My Route with the 94th Armored Field Artillery Battalion.

# CONTENTS

*Prologue* / *xi*

1 Jewish and a Christian Scientist / 1

2 Sign Me Up / 15

3 You're in the Army Now! / 24

4 Tests, Allies, and Enemies / 31

5 Going Nowhere / 41

6 Division Without a Mission / 52

7 I Ask for a Flask / 73

8 Don't Complain about Warm Beer / 82

9 I Begin Killing the Enemy / 109

10 "Abandon Post!" / 123

11 "I Am Going to Die" / 134

12 The Silence Is Hard on My Ears / 145

13 I Stop Writing Home / 152

**14**  It Gets to the Best of Us / 161

**15**  Ice Cream in Bed, Courtesy of
Patton / 168

**16**  The Motherland / 178

**17**  I Sleep in Hitler's Bed / 194

**18**  If the War Is Over, Why Are They Still
Shooting at Us? / 202

**19**  Home, Not So Sweet / 212

**20**  Return to the War Zone / 222

*Epilogue* / 232

*Acknowledgments* / 239

*Index* / 241

*Photographs follow pages 68, 102, and 234*

# PROLOGUE

*Though I walk through the valley of the shadow of death, I will fear no evil, for Thou art with me.*

**I PRAY EVERY MISERABLE NIGHT.** The war has changed me in ways that will take the better part of my life to understand, let alone make peace with. Don't ask me how. If you have to ask, you've never been to war.

Eleven months of anguish—that's what it's been, give or take. Sure, there are moments when you cut loose, when someone stumbles upon a cache of brandy and we play an extra round of poker. But the fear never leaves you. It's ever-present—a constant gnawing that has you wondering if you've said all the things you need to say to all the people you need to say things to. Because any given breath could be your last.

Nights can be agonizing. When you hear that ghastly whistle of an incoming mortar round . . . its eerie crescendo, increasing in intensity as it approaches—without a doubt the most awful sound I've ever heard. Here it comes. Only a few seconds before it's going to hit, barely enough time to grab your helmet and pray to whatever God you hope is still listening. So loud now, it's like a thousand shrieking pigs. And then the earth shakes—a geyser of stones, cards, and bodies. You exhale. Not your poker game. Not tonight.

Fifty yards away, a trio of aluminum dog tags is all that's left of three young men who were just like you ten seconds ago. Barely shaving, heartsick, terrified, numbing themselves behind an armor of bravado. By the luck of the draw, you'll live to see another day.

I myself lived another 25,600 days . . . but who's counting. In my mid-nineties now, I'm a dinosaur—one of the last men left standing in the last war we had any business fighting. At least that's how I see it.

Many of us died in the fields of France and Germany; others, later, on the battlefronts of life. By God's grace, I outlived most of them. And it's given me plenty of time to think—about what it all meant, whether it was worth it. I needed a good deal of hindsight and perspective to piece it all together; the rumination certainly didn't happen in the moment. There aren't many philosophers on a battlefield. The true magnitude of the nightmare doesn't sink in until much later. But there was one incident that shook the foundations of my being the instant it occurred. It hit me like a ton of bricks.

It was April 4, 1945. We were deep into Germany, and yet the Nazi army refused to surrender. In less than a month, Hitler would put a gun to his head and the war would end. Until that time, however, they kept fighting us tooth and nail, as if backed into a corner. The previous morning, my battalion had barely survived a vicious ambush on a bridge south of Gotha, and on this day it became clear why the Germans were fighting with such desperation—what they did not want us to see.

I was riding in a jeep behind that of my commanding officer, Bob Parker, only five years my senior and already a lieutenant colonel. A Harvard grad with an uncle who was a general, Parker exuded confidence, and I felt privileged to serve
under his command. At age twenty-three, I was a lieutenant
in the 94th Armored Field Artillery Battalion of Patton's
Third Army. My job was that of forward observer, the expend-
able officer who sneaks up close to the enemy to get a read on
their position and radios it back to the howitzers. But on this
crisp spring morning in 1945 I wasn't on the battlefield; I just
happened to be out in front with Parker as our combat command moved forward into newly conquered terrain. Everything seemed almost routine—until we approached the town
of Ohrdruf and passed a large residential structure in the
countryside, Bauhaus style and probably built in the 1930s,
complete with a moat. It struck us as slightly odd. A moat?

Tall trees screened a full view of whatever was on the other
side of the road. Parker glanced back at me—let's check it out.
We drove over the moat's bridge and parked. Parker grabbed
his carbine and I followed suit. We ventured inside the building. The interior was lavish. The wealthy German industri-
alist who owned the place was not present, but his servants
were and they seemed nervous as hell. We soon understood
why. It was plainly visible through the living room windows.

Parker and I dashed out of the house, our pulses racing.
What we saw was something no American had witnessed
up to that point. Surrounded by filth, we encountered a grim
spectacle, a huge pyramid-like stack of corpses, seeming-
ly murdered by shots to the head within the last few hours.
Nearly all the bodies had Jewish stars on their tattered "prison" uniforms. The ghastly scene still haunts me, the horror,

unspeakable. Why were we the first GIs to stumble upon this? God only knows. It's taken me a lifetime to come to terms with it.

I was shaken by that war, suffering from what they called "battle rattle" back then, "shell-shock" in World War I. (It took three more questionable wars before they gave it a clinical name: post-traumatic stress disorder—PTSD.)

It crept up on so many of us, and once it took hold, we were at its mercy. Perhaps by explaining my own experiences, others may be able to glean the lessons I wish desperately I had been able to learn back then. That's why I'm writing this, before it's too late: one of the last memoirs of World War II.

# 1

# JEWISH AND A
# CHRISTIAN SCIENTIST

**MY ARMY DOG TAGS HAD "C" ON THEM RATHER THAN "J,"** and no one seemed to recognize me as Jewish (nor did I bother to tell them). Starting around 1883, my maternal ancestors decided not to observe the Jewish faith, although they always recognized their Jewish origins. My great-grandmother Rachel Goldberg, who had emigrated to the United States in 1855 at the age of twenty-one, ended up with her family in Texarkana, Texas, where, in her fifties, she became a Christian Scientist. Mary Baker Eddy had founded the Church of Christ, Scientist in Boston only a few years before, in 1879. Christian Science posits that the material world is a mental construct, an illusion of sorts. True reality is spiritual, and we can tap into that field of infinite possibilities through prayer, which has the power to heal us of all ailments. Our tradition of practicing Christian Science meant, among other things, abstaining from seeing doctors, using medicine, drinking alcohol, or smoking tobacco.

An ardent believer, my great-grandmother became one of the first Christian Science "practitioners" in Texas. As a kind of spiritual medic, a practitioner attempts to help her patients through prayer. Rachel's three children—Louis, Mathilda, and Annie (my grandmother)—were all lifelong Christian Scientists, as was Annie's only child, my mother, Larie, who never drank or smoked and seldom saw a doctor. When she married my dad, Benjamin, he, too, became a Scientist and no longer attended Jewish services. Benjamin read the Bible and Mary Baker Eddy's *Science and Health with Key to the Scriptures*, known as "doing his lesson," almost every day of his life, and this practice gave him great pleasure and a sense of peace. But, unlike Larie, he did smoke occasionally (cigars and a pipe) and had a weekly Old Fashioned cocktail.

Like the generations before me, I was raised a Christian Scientist, studying Mary Baker Eddy's book and praying regularly. Without question a Jewish greenhorn, I knew absolutely nothing about the religion of my forebears. In 1933, the year Hitler came to power in Germany and began his government-sponsored program of anti-Semitism, I was an eighth-grader at Grant Grammar School in San Francisco, an especially liberal city, where different religious and ethnic groups got along famously. I was protected by a strong democratic government, which I took entirely for granted.

That year I won the American Legion Award for best male student, probably because I did well acting in the school's plays and did even better at debating, an activity I loved. The main subject being debated that year at Grant Grammar was whether or not capital punishment should be abolished, and I became a lifelong opponent of the death penalty after my dad introduced me to his friend James Johnston, the former warden of San Quentin State Penitentiary (and soon to become the first warden of Alcatraz).

From his firsthand experience seeing dozens of men executed by hanging, Warden Johnston became convinced that capital punishment was an abomination. His descriptions of the ordeal—the looks of desperation or sudden remorse, the twitching bodies—filled my thirteen-year-old mind with horror and a conviction that human life was sacrosanct. I fought hard to win my grammar school debates on the subject of abolishing the death penalty. But debating involves being able to argue both points of view, and I'd often find myself on the other side of the argument. I was decidedly uncomfortable if I won those fights.

To me as an eighth-grader, the world seemed black and white, and wanton killing was always wrong. In less than ten years, I'd be taking other men's lives without hesitation, my innocence gone forever. But I was a Boy Scout back then, quite literally. A proud member of Grant School's Troop 100, I enjoyed the outdoor activities, especially camping, yet I never quite made Eagle Scout, the defining measure of success in scouting. Whether it was a lack of focus or ambition, this was a sign, I feel sure, of the rocky career paths that were to plague me in the army and beyond.

One of my first "careers" was delivering *Saturday Evening Post* magazines. As part of my job, I had to make deliveries on Filbert Street, two blocks south of the Cow Hollow neighborhood where I lived. The kids on the Filbert Street block, some of whom I knew and had always liked, suddenly started calling out in a derisive manner when I came by with my magazines: "Hey, there's the rabbi." At first I didn't know what they were referring to. The word "rabbi" meant nothing to me, a student at a Christian Science Sunday school. However, when I mentioned this teasing to my parents, they were distressed; they explained that the Filbert Street kids were Catholics and I was not. I had never considered that a difference in ideology or belief could be a cause for disliking someone—still less, that I might be the one being disliked. I can only guess that their parents must have made some comment about my family's Jewishness.

I experienced discrimination again on an even greater level in my first dancing class, a private affair not connected with my grammar school, which included both gentile and Jewish kids. I enjoyed attending and loved dancing with the girls in the class. But when the second year of the class came around, all Jewish students were excluded. This time I got the message clearly on my own: if you're Jewish, get lost. These combined experiences gave me a taste of the cruelty caused by narrow-minded beliefs.

Not long after my exclusion from the dance hall, my father, a gentle, unaggressive person, strongly recommended that I learn to box. He first had me take lessons from Spider Roach, a former lightweight champion, and later from a boxing pro at our apartment at 2100 Pacific Avenue. I would put on boxing gloves and a leather helmet, and my instructors would teach me how to stand with my left leg and arm in front, how to balance, how to protect myself, and how to deliver blows. It was a confidence-building sport, even though I wasn't a natural boxer. I don't recall ever hitting anybody in anger before or after these classes. And I always wondered why my father was so much in favor of my taking boxing lessons. Obviously, he wanted me to learn how to protect myself, but as I remained naive about the violence that religious prejudice can instill, I had no idea who he thought might put me in danger.

Around this same time, the subject of Hitler came up at our dinner table. My mother, Larie, though eighteen years younger than my mild-mannered father, was not shy about expressing her political opinions, especially on the subject of German aggression and expansionism. A year after graduating from Bryn Mawr College in 1916, she had gone to work for the United States Committee on Public Information, which was essentially a wartime propaganda machine. The U.S. had waited on the sidelines as a neutral observer until the final year of the "Great War." So when Woodrow Wilson finally decided to commit our troops to the blood-drenched battlefield (which had already taken millions of lives), he needed to rally the American public. To lead the effort, the president enlisted investigative journalist George Creel. My mom was one of the college graduates who got jobs with this campaign. She and her colleagues were asked to research our foes and find ways of casting them in a negative light—that is, to get the lowdown on Kaiser Wilhelm II or anyone else who could be caricatured and ridiculed in the press. It was no great stretch to portray the German enemy as barbaric. When I studied the war in school, I was made supremely aware of how the German side had violated the "rules of war" by using mustard gas, a chemical weapon, and torpedoing a passenger ship, the *Lusitania*, killing almost 2,000 civilians. But what I didn't learn in my history class was that our side had used chemical weapons, too. Nor did I learn that the *Lusitania*'s hold had been secretly filled with weapons and ammunition to supply the British war effort, so it was not strictly a "civilian" ship.

Propaganda has always been a part of warfare. In order to persuade an army that the enemy deserves to be annihilated, we dehumanize them and convince the public that they are evil. We give them names—"kraut," "gook," "towel-head"—to mock their worth and make it easier for our soldiers to pull their triggers, because killing another human being is not in our nature. Collectively, we must adjust our moral standards to the highly abnormal conditions of wartime—but it takes a toll on us, both as a nation and individually. This stark lesson would soon be hitting me like a sledgehammer on the front lines of World War II, where some 60 million people would soon die, making it three times more deadly than its predecessor.

But World War I was hardly a picnic. By the time all was said and done, about 17 million people died between 1914 and 1918 on the battlefields of Europe, making the First World War one of the deadliest conflicts in human history. It became known as "The War to End All Wars"—yet that prognostication lasted hardly even one generation.

By the time I entered high school, Hitler was laying out his vision for a Third Reich. My mother, with her training in the propaganda office, saw the writing on the wall, and frequently shared her theories of Hitler's bellicose intentions at our dinner table. I took everything she said as gospel truth, so I was a little surprised when, in 1935, she proposed an extended European vacation. Maybe she wanted to see things for herself, or simply show me the continent, before it was too late. Indeed, in every country visited by our entourage (my great-aunt and grandmother joined us in Paris and accompanied us on some of the trip) there was an undercurrent of danger, a foreboding sense of imminent doom.

Following the Nazi seizure of power in 1933, Hitler had established the Reich Ministry of Public Enlightenment and Propaganda headed by Joseph Goebbels. The ministry's aim was to communicate the Nazi message through art, music, theater, films, books, radio, educational materials, and the press. It was the Nazi counterpart to the U.S. Committee on Public Information (where my mother had worked)—but I never saw these agencies as having any sort of equivalency. The vitriol and hate spewing from the Nazis' side were truly horrifying. It began with newspaper articles on "Solving the Jewish Question," like this one published in 1933:

> As a result of the victory of the National Socialist revolution, the Jewish Question has become a problem for those who never before thought about solving the Jewish Question. Everyone has seen that the current situation is intolerable. Allowing free development and equality for the Jews has led to an "unfree" situation of exploited competition, and to a handing over of important positions within the German people to those of a foreign race.

Less than a year later, the tone had risen to a fevered pitch, as in this 1934 banner headline printed in blood red by the Nazi weekly *Der Stürmer:* "Jewish Murder Plan against Gentile Humanity Revealed." The article went on to accuse Jews of practicing ritual killings to secure the blood of Christians for use in Jewish religious rituals. By the time we arrived in Europe in 1935, political cartoons were ubiquitous in the German press, featuring large-nosed, money-grubbing caricatures of people like me, with captions along these lines: "The Jew's symbol is a worm, not without reason. He seeks to creep up on what he wants."

We were appalled. While my mother had heard chilling stories about the mood in Europe, now we were seeing it with our own eyes. In Vienna, a charming and well-placed Jewish couple took us out to a nice dinner, but it was hard to enjoy our food. The conversation quickly turned to their great fear of the future because of what was taking place in Nazi Germany. They felt unsafe in their Austrian homeland but did not know what to do. (They had every right to be terrified; within a few short years, the Gestapo would arrive in Vienna to round up all the Jews for imprisonment in concentration camps and likely execution.)

In Warsaw, we saw Polish military everywhere and were told they were preparing to defend Poland from foreign enemies. And again, history bore out their fears when the country was ravaged by both Nazi Germany and the Soviet Union.

In the Soviet Union, which we visited upon leaving Poland, my mother and I shared a train compartment with Louis Fischer, a correspondent who covered the USSR for *The Nation*, along with a young American PhD student from Princeton and two Soviet army officers. Fischer told us that the Soviets felt that Hitler was bad news and would soon be attacking them, and that Stalin was therefore quietly rearming. At one stop, the American graduate student was suddenly arrested by USSR police and removed from the train. We left the station about thirty minutes later without the student and never saw him again. I have often wondered what happened to the poor fellow.

We had planned to tour Germany as our final stop, but my mother had second thoughts. Not only did she nix the visit, she refused even to cross the border. We drove forty-eight miles out of our way over a difficult mountain road through the Italian Dolomites to avoid taking an easy shortcut through Germany. Larie was simply unwilling to set foot in the Nazi stronghold.

If my trip to Europe were not enough to scare me about Hitler and his Third Reich, two events in San Francisco—neither of any particular political significance but definitely vivid in my own mind—reinforced my fears. The first was the assignment of a Nazi of considerable notoriety as the German consul general in San Francisco. His official residence was but one city block from where I lived. Ordinarily my family paid no attention as German consul generals came and went, but Baron Manfred von Killinger, who arrived in San Francisco in 1936, was a different story. An early member of the Nazi party, he was known far and wide for his virulent anti-Semitism; in 1941 he would be placed in charge of the Nazis' extermination program for Jews and Gypsies in Romania. But in 1936–37 he was my neighbor and, though I never saw or met him, I was always aware of how close I was to an evil human being and I avoided going by his house at all costs. I couldn't bear even to look at it.

The second event, personally arranged by Baron von Killinger, was the arrival in San Francisco in 1937 of a brand-new German warship, the *Admiral Graf Spee,* a heavy cruiser that the Germans referred to as a "pocket battleship," meaning a warship that met the naval limitations on size and armaments established by the victors of World War I. With some degree of trepidation I went on board to see this ship and found it scary: all the rooms had polished swastikas on their walls and the larger rooms had photographs of Adolf Hitler in the most prominent places. I found it oppressive and kept thinking of what would happen to me if those smiling midshipmen ever got their hands on me. I envisioned being beaten and imprisoned, and I fled the ship without looking back.

In 1938, when I entered Stanford, I was probably one of the most anti-Nazi students on an American college campus. I'd been following the pre-war scene in Europe closely and had concluded that, strategically, the odds were in France and Britain's favor; France had a strong advantage with its Maginot Line underground defense and Britain had a well-trained army. I could not have been more wrong in my evaluations. Both the Maginot Line and the British army turned out to be of little military value against the prodigious German military machine, which exerted absolute dominance on the battlefield. (I'd soon be experiencing this for myself.) They were better trained than we were, their guns were more powerful, and their tanks had better armor. If Britain's Royal Air Force hadn't stopped the Luftwaffe cold in the 1940 Battle of Britain, England might have fallen under Nazi control like the rest of Western Europe.

As in World War I, the Americans would join the conflict fairly late in the game. Knowing what I knew about the Nazis, I couldn't believe that we would remain sitting idly on the sidelines after the war began. As a fan of Franklin D. Roosevelt, who made it clear that he thought we should help the British, I was strongly in favor of the U.S. supporting Great Britain in its war against Germany. But I found myself out of step with many of my fellow students at Stanford, most of whom were disinterested in events taking place far from our shores. And opposition to getting involved in the war was getting stronger.

In late 1940 a chapter of the America First Committee, a new, adamantly isolationist organization, sprang up on campus and made fast headway. It had been started earlier that fall at Yale Law School and quickly grew to over 800,000 dues-paying members. In San Francisco the German American Bund, which had been around since 1933, was successfully touting the bond between the United States and Nazi Germany. There is no doubt that our involvement in World War I had sapped many Americans' enthusiasm for further involvement in a foreign war. I was disheartened. But my political opinions were not the only things that isolated me on campus. I was shocked to find in my freshman year that a form of anti-Semitism was practiced openly at Stanford (as it was at many universities across the country): its fraternities and sororities were closed to Jewish males and females.

Most freshmen with social aspirations sought membership in these coveted institutions. When I saw my gentile friends being "rushed" while I was excluded, it cast a shadow in my mind. Though the overall attitude at Stanford was broad-minded, the exclusionary policies of Fraternity Row rankled. This taste of injustice embittered me and increased my desire to help England fight Hitler, the biggest anti-Semite anywhere. Even though most of America was not with me, I became more determined than ever to cross that pond and join the battlefield in Europe.

. . .

Though the frats had slammed the door in my face, there was one unit at Stanford that was happy to have me: ROTC. I had started a "Reserve Officers' Training Corps" program some years back at Galileo High School and enjoyed it. The ROTC choices at Stanford were "Field Artillery" and "Ordnance," the latter primarily for engineering students. Not being an engineer, I chose field artillery, which had an added bonus for me: horses. I had started riding when I was six and my parents took me to a resort in New Mexico; I had asthma at the time and they thought I would feel better—which I did. The resort had lots of horses, and my dad took me riding, showing me how to hang on to the western saddle's pommel. When I was old enough for summer camp, the ones chosen for me were in the Sierras with plenty of horseback riding, and over time I became a competent rider. So I was happy to discover that field artillery in Stanford's ROTC program was a horse-drawn affair.

The artillery pieces they used were 75-millimeter howitzers (field guns), last used in World War I and long obsolete by 1939, but I didn't mind one bit because they were deployed using horses. In fact, I loved the riding part much more than the artillery part. Our three ROTC instructors, all regular army officers (as distinct from reserve ones), were accomplished equestrians. The top-ranker was Colonel Henry B. Allen, an avuncular, pleasant man given to making speeches, which no one paid attention to. The middle-ranking officer was Major LeCount Slocum, who always seemed to be scolding, and I gave him a wide a berth. The junior officer was Captain Roger Goldsmith, my favorite—a stickler for rules and regulations, but warm and helpful.

I remember once, on an overnight drill in open country behind Stanford, we were marching dog-tired with rifles and backpacks to the mess area, which was still miles away (where our horses were I have no idea)—and it was raining, to boot—when we came across our three officer-teachers, all comfortably seated at a sheltered table, eating lunch and being waited on by enlisted men. As I passed Captain Goldsmith (who smiled at me), I said, "Sir, how come you have it so easy and we don't?"—to which he replied matter-of-factly: "RHIP, Boas." I didn't even know what it meant back then. A few years later, I'd be well aware of its meaning and I'd be making damn sure to take full advantage of it: Rank Has Its Privileges.

. . .

By mid-March of 1939, Hitler rolled into Czechoslovakia, virtually unopposed. He was already in control of Austria, and on September 1 attacked Poland, soon after making a nonaggression deal with Stalin. Two days later, France and England declared war on Germany, but they were unable to stop his advance into Poland. Indeed, the next year was disastrous for the Allies. Hitler conquered France and along the way captured Denmark, Norway, Belgium, Luxembourg, and the Netherlands. When he defeated the British troops in France, they were forced to evacuate as best they could back to England. He then went after the English with his air force, the Luftwaffe. Had this effort succeeded, it would have been all over for democracy in Europe. I felt with fervor that we should be joining the fight. And yet I soon found myself arguing passionately—and very publicly—for the opposing viewpoint.

Late in 1940, I stood at a lectern in front of an audience of one hundred at the College (now University) of Puget Sound. With four other members of the Stanford debate team, I had taken the train to Tacoma the night before. It was a very competitive tournament, with colleges from all over the country. This was the final round against Pepperdine, and I had to make my team's last statement.

Being the last to speak tested my persuasive abilities—it required carefully summarizing and underscoring every argument we had made so the judges would have no choice but to vote in our favor. The topic in this case was the question of the day: should America commit troops to the escalating conflict in Europe?

Our team, to my chagrin, had been assigned to argue the negative. But my love of debate trumped my personal views on the matter, as it should. And so I fired away, giving argument after argument on why it would be folly for us to join the war: we were not directly threatened, our army was unprepared, the cost would be staggering, and so on. There was a lot of truth to what I was saying. While Germany had been spending a fortune developing its military technology, most of our weapons dated from World War I. While their panzers were state-of-the-art, American servicemen were more comfortable riding on horses than riding in tanks. This mismatch would cost us dearly. I would soon be seeing it up close and personal, losing good friends and very nearly losing myself.

But that future seemed far away as I delivered my isolationist tirade that afternoon. After I wrapped up my argument, the audience broke into thunderous applause. The judges, if not already convinced, noted the populist vote. And we walked home with the trophy.

I gazed out at the Pacific in a bittersweet mood, as the coastal train chugged south to Palo Alto. Hitler clearly wanted to rule the world. Why was no one else feeling the way I did about this madman?

# 2

# SIGN ME UP

**ON DECEMBER 7, 1941,** I was driving a most attractive colleague, Nancy Burkett, from San Francisco to Palo Alto. It was not a date; I had no girlfriends back then. Nancy was a classmate and we were driving to attend a Sunday morning seminar at a professor's home. Though I didn't have a sweetheart, at least I had a car—thanks to the fact that my dad ran a local Pontiac dealership. I was proud of my Silver Streak coupe (on loan from my dad), with its sleek styling and horizontal grille. We were listening to big band music on the AM radio, when suddenly the program was interrupted by an urgent announcement: America was under attack.

In a sneak raid—for which our military forces were not prepared—Japanese fighter planes had all but destroyed our Pacific fleet at Pearl Harbor. We listened in abject horror. I felt outraged. Defiant. Saddened. Helpless.

The next day President Roosevelt, in a speech to Congress, declared war on Japan—but, it is important to note, *not* on Germany. Despite Hitler's unchecked aggressions against his neighbors, Roosevelt was still dealing with a reluctant Congress when it came to moving into the European theater of war. I idolized Franklin D. Roosevelt during this stage of his career, and I found his proclamation of war speech absolutely inspiring. But I was still dismayed that we were focused on Asia, not Europe, where, in my mind, the deeper threat lay. And then, four days later, on December 11, 1941, an extraordinary thing happened: Hitler declared war on *us*. If he had not done so, the United States might never have gotten involved in the war in Europe.

As I saw it, Hitler was making a fatal mistake. Happily for the democracies, this was the third in a series of bad decisions by Hitler. The first was not regrouping after losing the air battle with Britain, to try to make a successful land invasion of England. The second was attacking the Soviet Union, which no one—not even Napoleon—had been able to defeat.

Hitler was a political genius, but his genius was flawed. And thank God for that—if it hadn't been, the Second World War might have ended very differently. With my ROTC artillery training, I was eager to do my part to defeat this tyrant. But there were several obstacles to overcome. First one: my mother.

Larie, as mentioned, was an anti-Nazi to the nth degree. She felt Hitler was so bad (and this was *before* anyone had any knowledge of the concentration camps) that he needed to be removed from the scene, no matter what the cost. But her idea of paying that cost, it turned out, did not include taking the life of her only child—i.e., me. An only child herself, she would have done anything to keep me off the battlefield, given the chance to do so. And I, foolishly, gave her just such a chance.

Although I had been a political science major, I'd taken an accounting course as a senior at Stanford. So in February 1942, to my surprise, I was offered not one but *two* commissions in the army, one in the field artillery, which I had earned by taking ROTC, and one as a lieutenant in the army's Finance Corps (the army apparently needing finance officers as much as it needed field artillery ones). I felt I was a field artilleryman, not a financial type, and so being in the Finance Corps held no appeal for me.

My parents had no knowledge of the dual offers I had received, and if I had followed the adage of "what they don't know won't hurt them," all would have been well. But I made the mistake of telling them, and it became an enormous scene in the living room of my parents' beautiful apartment on Pacific Avenue in San Francisco. Larie implored me to choose the safety of the Finance Corps. Because my mom loathed Hitler and prayed daily for his defeat, I had thought she would have been proud to see me take a crack at getting rid of him as a member of the field artillery. I might add that if women of her age (she was then forty-eight) had been allowed to fight in World War II, I feel sure she would have gone into combat without hesitation. But she couldn't bear the thought of losing her only child. Choosing between shooting guns or sitting behind a desk was a no-brainer: choose the desk! She became rather hysterical, in fact, pleading with me almost on bended knee. I felt very sorry for my mother, and though I understood how she felt, I knew there was nothing I could do to relieve her anxiety short of rejecting the position I was entirely set on taking. My father wisely realized that Larie needed some space and escorted me quickly to the door. Leaving my mother disconsolate, I took off with my dad to his club.

My father had remained relatively quiet during the titanic clash between my mom and me. His demeanor on the issue was entirely different. A calm and physically courageous person, he spoke to me when we were driving to the club and asked where I thought I could do the most good: finance or artillery. When I said the field artillery, he said, "Then that's where you belong." I have always cherished this particular memory of him. Dad and I were close, and we both knew he was taking a big risk—I was his only child, too.

My mother, meanwhile, would spend the entire war dreading that every phone call or piece of mail might be the one telling her of my demise. Neither of us ever quite forgot this confrontation. It was a factor in a shift in my relationship with my mother, which up until then had been a very positive one.

Having made my choice to enlist in the artillery, I went blithely to an air force medical center near Stanford to take the physical exam that I was required to pass in order to be eligible for a commission. After undressing, I took my place at the back of a long line of civilian applicants, and when my turn finally arrived, I faced a pleasant air force medical corpsman who asked me a bunch of questions and noted my answers on a notepad. When he inquired if I had had any childhood diseases, I had to pause for a minute as I was unsure. I didn't know what illnesses I might have had because, as a Christian Scientist, I had almost never seen a doctor. Health problems were worked on by Mrs. Jacobs, my Christian Science practitioner, and were seldom discussed in medical terms. As I sat there staring at the corpsman, no warning bells went off in my mind, and I decided to proffer a minor health issue, which I had suddenly recalled: some problems with childhood asthma (which my Christian Science practitioner had worked to help me eliminate). Feeling like an exemplary American, I casually told the medical corpsman, "I only had asthma when I was a small child, and I've long outgrown it." Big mistake.

I had no idea how a sickness like asthma was regarded in the military; I just wanted to be a good fellow and please the smiling corpsman. What I did not realize was that I might just as well have said: "I have only had a touch of leprosy." The army did not want asthmatics, especially in its officer corps. This was a time when I should have remained quiet, smiled back at the corpsman, and said nothing.

Two weeks after the smiling corpsman made his notes on a pad, I went to the Stanford post office to get my mail and there in my postal box was an official-looking envelope with a letter that carried a devastating blow. It was from the army adjutant general, a major general, no less, informing me that the offer of a field artillery commission was withdrawn—"due to history of asthma in childhood."

Reading and re-reading the letter, I felt crushed. Here I was, a person in excellent physical condition, being treated as if I were entirely unable to function. At age twenty, I hadn't had any trace of asthma since I was about eight or nine. I was rowing on Stanford's crew team at the time, a sport that required high levels of stamina and strength. At this momentous time, with the future of the planet at stake—when we certainly needed every able-bodied man in order to stop the Nazi juggernaut—I was being shut out for no good reason. That's when the anger set in, and anger can be a great motivator for me. I let the panic go and started focusing on seizing control of the situation.

I decided that the first thing to do was to go see two people I held in high regard: Mrs. Maude V. Jacobs, my Christian Science practitioner, a dear, sweet, loving lady, white-haired and small in stature, who would sit in a room with me and close her eyes and pray, and Colonel Henry Allen, my ROTC commander, an imposing and authoritative figure on a huge black horse. President Roosevelt could turn for help to Secretary of War Henry L. Stimson or Secretary of State Cordell Hull. I was going to place my bets on the team of Jacobs and Allen. (My initial thought, I confess, had been to write to the Commander in Chief himself in hopes that my idol might personally intervene on my behalf, but I had to move fast, and getting the attention of President Roosevelt, with wars on two fronts, might have been a bit of a stretch.) So I turned to my religion for help and called Mrs. Jacobs.

I had met Mrs. Jacobs in 1926, when I was five. For years, she would come to sit by my bedside at our home on Broderick Street in San Francisco to pray for me to overcome whatever ailed me. I trusted her fully and never felt that my trust was misplaced. And when I called her in January 1942, sixteen years after we first met, she went right to work. After expressing her indignation about the army's decision, she prayed that the ruling be overturned. The power of prayer to us Christian Scientists knows no bounds. It can heal body, mind, and soul, and certainly it has the power to affect the mind of an adjutant general and persuade him to reverse the bureaucratic decision of a subordinate.

I felt good about our prayer session, but I wanted to bolster my efforts by going through official channels as well. Thus, following my prayer session with Mrs. Jacobs, I went to see my old ROTC boss, Colonel Allen, who also expressed outrage and pledged to do everything in his power to get the decision reversed. The colonel suggested that I respond in writing to the adjutant general and tell him that I was a well-trained field artilleryman in excellent physical shape. Though I had great respect for Colonel Allen's judgment, I didn't feel overly optimistic about the efficacy of a simple plea letter to the very person who had disqualified me. Being a debater, I knew I needed supporting evidence to buttress my case.

What if I got a second opinion from a doctor of my own? There was only one problem—as a Christian Scientist, I didn't know any doctors. Actually that wasn't entirely true. There was Dr. Aaron Green, my eye doctor and a great family friend, who had treated me for being cockeyed by having me watch a large revolving wheel. Then I remembered that, as a kid, I had also secretly seen a physician named Dr. Edward Matzger. A highly respected allergist, Dr. Matzger had given me allergy shots when I was a child, and eventually my asthma disappeared, whether because of the shots or prayer we never quite determined—although, truthfully, I always favored the prayer. (My parents and I hid the fact that I had visited him from Mrs. Jacobs.)

As soon as the idea of contacting Dr. Matzger entered my consciousness (perhaps it had been prayer-inspired), I felt confident that it would be my ticket to reinstatement. Sure enough, when I told Dr. Matzger of my army commission predicament, he tested me and found me without any suggestion of asthma. I then did what Colonel Allen had suggested and wrote a letter to the army adjutant general, including with it the report from Dr. Matzger verifying that I was indeed healthy. My letter concluded:

It is my own personal belief that I can best serve the interests of my country through a position in the field artillery in which I am best qualified by reason of past training, capacity, and desire, and I hope it will be possible for me to be commissioned in the United States Army.

I put the letter in the mail and waited for a reply. The waiting seemed interminable. I was buoyed by Mrs. Jacobs's encouraging comments during the two weeks in which I literally sweated out a response from the army. "God will protect you," she kept telling me. Every day I approached the Stanford post office with trepidation. And then one morning, after two weeks had come and gone, I walked into the post office without particularly thinking about my problem. Dialing the combination on my mailbox, I spotted a large manila envelope, which was all curled up, and pulled it out. When I smoothed it out, I saw it was addressed to "2nd Lt. John R. Boas, AUS." Who's he? I wondered. (I never used my given name, only my middle name, Roger.) And why the "AUS"? "Army of the United States." And then it dawned on me: wonder of wonders, I had been accepted. My relief and joy knew no bounds. A letter from Major General James A. Ulio, the adjutant general, dated May 15, 1942, began, "By direction of the President you are appointed and commissioned in the Army of the United States," and ended with: "The physical defects, history of bronchial asthma in childhood, are waived."

Little did I know then that in 1945, almost three years later to the day, I would be pulled out of combat by our battalion surgeon to be hospitalized in Luxembourg City with a serious bronchial attack; and that I would find none other than General George S. Patton standing by my bedside and wishing me well. But for now, in 1942, my slip-of-the-tongue nightmare was over. Whether I would be sent to fight Emperor Hirohito's troops in the Far East or Adolf Hitler's forces in Europe I had no idea. All I could think was: Bless General Ulio, and Mrs. Jacobs, and Colonel Allen. I was in!

# 3

# YOU'RE IN
# THE ARMY NOW!

**WHEN I SAID I WAS A BOY SCOUT I MEANT IT.** Before the army, I didn't smoke, drink, hardly swore, and hadn't even had a real girl-friend. Man, would that change. The day after graduating, I was already in uniform.

Having been sworn into the army a week earlier, I exchanged a college campus for Camp Roberts, a large un-landscaped army post of 47,000 acres located about halfway between San Francisco and Los Angeles on Highway 101, near the town of Paso Robles. Not particularly attractive, it consisted of hundreds of two-story wooden barracks that housed, fed, and educated about 20,000 men a month. The officers' barracks were surprisingly comfortable; two of us junior officers shared an agreeably sized room, with about twenty-four rooms in an officers' barrack. Roberts had kitchens, mess halls, and a store run by the army where basic essentials could be purchased, all housed in lookalike buildings. The only building on the

24

post with any individuality—and it didn't look like much—was the officers' club.

Roberts was a place where men fresh from civilian life were taught to adjust to the rules of the military in thirty days of academics, drills, plus the socializing that occurs when a bunch of men are crowded together for long periods of time. Camaraderie was a big part of it, but I waded into that part with caution and a bit of condescension. I quickly formed strong opinions about my colleagues: to me, they were socially inept and lacking in intellect. The wives, whom I met at cocktail parties, were sweet and nice but said very little. At the time I put it down to the mores of people I regarded as country folk. On June 21, 1942, I wrote home:

> All of the officers are college men, but few, if any, appear to be intellectuals or men of breeding. Consequently they lack all but the elementary social graces. . . . The mess is a grim affair with no conversation at the table except "pass the butter, etc.," no introductions, and the like. . . . Friday, my battalion gave a cocktail party for our battalion commander . . . believe it or not none of us new officers were introduced to the colonel; no attempt at formal conversation was made, and the affair was deadly. Just lack of savoir-faire on the part of the local talent.

Undoubtedly, I had an inflated sense of my own worth. My background was neither exalted nor distinguished. My father was a nonintellectual middle-class San Franciscan who never went to college but who, nonetheless, married his opposite: an intelligent upper-middle-class girl from Bryn Mawr College. My grades at Stanford were mediocre. Clearly, I had no right to belittle anyone. But that didn't stop me from describing the bulk of my fellow officers as clodhoppers. Looking back now, I know for certain this was a defense mechanism on my part. It was a man's world—lots of men in very close quarters. Something entirely unfamiliar to me.

Prior to my service, I had been surrounded by women—an only child, cosseted by my mother, grandmother, great-aunt, and my mother's close female friends for most of my life. And I've wondered if this cosseting caused me to never rise higher than first lieutenant during almost four years of service; most of my Roberts colleagues reached captain status, while a small number achieved the rank of major or even lieutenant colonel. They moved up in rank because as kids they had no choice but to work harder than I did; if they wanted something, they had to plan how to get it. I didn't have to plan; I only had to ask.

Even during my time in training I was spoiled. I expected presents, and presents I got from family and family friends from the time I entered the service in June 1942 until I got out in November 1945. The flow started in Camp Roberts: candy from Blum's (a famous San Francisco confectioner) sent by my grandmother, nuts and dried fruit sent by a writer friend of my mother's—all this, and I hadn't been in the army thirty days.

And I had visitors, too. Most of the officers in training at Roberts came from afar and so had no contact with their families; I, on the other hand, hailed from San Francisco, only 200 miles away. So, sure enough, one weekend my mother, father, and grandmother all came down to Paso Robles to visit me. Strange to say, or perhaps not so strange, I loved being with them. Here I was, twenty years old, an officer in the army on active duty training for combat, and I slipped easily into my old role of adored son and grandson.

I was innocent still. Not realizing, perhaps, that it was time for me to shift my allegiance to my new family: the army. It was urgent, in fact, for me to do so. The stakes would soon be life and death. I needed to be bonded on the deepest level to the man next to me, and he to me: one for all, and all for one. It was the only way for us to survive the madness. But there remained some hesitation on my part. Or maybe it was fear.

Don't get me wrong. I enjoyed the companionship of many of my fellow second lieutenants: I found at least a dozen to be decent, charming, and good-humored. They came from various parts of the country: lots from Colorado, almost as many from Georgia, and quite a few from Utah and Nebraska. I had met some of the Coloradoans at a mandatory two-week ROTC exercise at Camp Ord in Monterey, California, a year earlier, and liked them a lot. There were three brothers with the surname Walt (another Walt brother was commanding a regiment of marines in the Pacific), and we became fast friends upon meeting again at Fort Sill, where we artillery officers would receive our field training. The Walts and others from Colorado were some of the nicest people I ever met. The Southerners from Georgia had a different style, however. Combative and full of wisecracks, they were the student officer group most anxious to enter combat. All of us would visit one another for hours on end in our rooms, asking the questions we were most anxious about: What was in store for us? Where would we end up? What would life be like? How long would the war go on? How would it change us?

Socializing at Roberts was every day and all the time, which represented quite a change for me. I had been something of a loner in college, a non-fraternity man living in a dormitory. Now I was surrounded by my brother officers, whom I interacted with in our barracks, classroom, mess hall, and at the officers' club. What particularly fascinated me was that so many were married, since my friends from home and from Stanford were still single, and I had yet to have a girlfriend. But these lieutenants hailed from different climes, where early marriage was de rigueur.

There was one demographic at Roberts with whom I had no contact: enlisted men. Truth be told, this was a matter of subconscious relief for me, as the question of how exactly to deal with them was a nagging anxiety for me. An officer's job is to command, not mingle, but I still feared being unable to relate. I had no interaction with enlisted personnel until later, and there I found that my fears were justified: I didn't know how to connect with them.

My letters home (and I wrote home a lot, at length) suggest I was far from complacent when it came to academics. I had a good mind and I knew how to listen and ask our instructors the right questions. I was absorbing a lot of information, probably more than most. I studied hard, was ambitious to succeed, and got good grades—with one glaring exception that almost did me in.

The classes for officers were not large, and the atmosphere was relaxed and informal, although the work being discussed was taken seriously. Each class had about thirty-five brand-new second lieutenants taught by a captain. I loved my continued study of gunnery, the most fascinating of the courses, and did well on the math that got the firepower to the target. I was also reasonably good at reading maps. I enjoyed "Weaponry and Tactics," but I couldn't read an aerial photo to save my life and found "Motor Transport" incomprehensible. I was a horseman.

Horses had served the field artillery well in World War I and were one reason I had taken ROTC at Stanford, where I had become reasonably expert in the use of horse-drawn 75mm howitzers. It was good training, but by 1942 the army had stopped using horses and the 75mm howitzer had been replaced by mobile 105mm howitzers. With the horses gone, instead of learning how to care for these wonderful animals, we became students of the internal combustion engine.

While I understood the need for it to be part of our training, it was by far my worst subject. As the son of an automobile dealer, all this should have come easily to me, but I never could comprehend what actually made cars run. Driving the four-ton trucks was enjoyable, but listening to lectures about repairing caster, camber, and brake deficiencies was Greek to me. While I found car repair, much less tank maintenance, impossible to understand, it was critical to my training—in modern mechanized warfare, it is absolutely vital to keep vehicles operational, tanks included. A stalled column is a doomed column, inviting enemy bombardment and ambush.

As bad as I was at working with vehicles, I ended up doing extremely well in handling weapons and quickly learned how to disassemble, reassemble, and shoot pistols, carbines, rifles, and machine guns. The one weapon that I struggled to learn to handle properly was the 37mm anti-tank gun, which I did not properly master until I was in combat. But I graduated from Roberts labeled a "sharpshooter," and on several occasions in combat I couldn't afford to be anything else.

When the thirty days at Camp Roberts were over, many of the officers, especially the infantry officers, went directly to the units they would serve in for the rest of the war. The artillery officers like me, however, were sent to Fort Sill in Oklahoma for three months or more of intensive training to acquire all the skills necessary to handle cannon fire. We'd be graduating to the 105mm howitzers, which were considerably more powerful than the 75mm guns to which I was accustomed, and where the slightest error could spell disaster. Indeed, the stakes would be amped up across the board. You failed at Sill, they could (and would) revoke your commission.

# 4

# TESTS, ALLIES, AND ENEMIES

**FORT SILL WAS TOUTED AS THE BE-ALL,** end-all of the field artillery. Opened in 1869, this installation had been around since the time of Buffalo Bill, and once claimed Geronimo as a guest (actually, he'd been there under a form of "house arrest"). Walking the grounds filled me with excitement. Compared to the barrenness of Roberts, Sill had appealing landscaping, with ubiquitous greenery: trees, lawns, flowers, plus a handsome swimming pool at a well-designed officers' club. There was an air of pomp and prestige to the place. I was equally taken by the people.

While Camp Roberts had expanded my social horizons, the sheer diversity and numbers at Sill represented a whole different ball game; I was simply fascinated by the smorgasbord of people. Men hailed from the Deep South, the Midwest, and Latin America. But within my class of sixty at Sill (officially called Battery Officers Class #65), there were only two black officers. The remaining African Americans on campus were all enlisted men, orderlies, and mess attendants. Many found this class division to be entirely appropriate. Negative views of blacks were palpable at Sill, especially among some of the Southerners, and the fact that the army remained segregated throughout the war did nothing to ease this. I wrote an angry letter home on August 14, 1942:

> They [the Southerners] think that Negros are dirt and that they are the "blessed." . . . We have several Negro officers here and, needless to say, the Southerners avoid them, despise them, and won't sit at the same mess table with them.

One of the Southern officers from Georgia routinely harassed and berated the black waiting staff (all of the waiters at Sill were black). One time, after this officer had given a very frightened waiter a particularly unpleasant dressing-down, this huge ex-football player from Nebraska, one Lieutenant Keefe, grabbed the Georgian by the neck, shook him vigorously, and said, "If you ever try to mistreat this waiter again, I'm going to knock you from one end of the mess to the other." Keefe became my instant hero.

I had little context for this tension between blacks and whites, nor had my family dwelt much on the subject of racial equality. But, thanks to Adolf Hitler, I was becoming a good deal more sensitive to racial matters. However, I was no saint, and communicated my own racist attitude in a letter to my parents:

> We were given colored troops on the march to work with, and when we reached our bivouac at 2 A.M. . . . all got out

their dice (called "galloping dominoes") and played craps until reveille at 5:30 next morning. I really like them—they are like great big children and go to sleep on you at a moment's notice.

Some of the trainees came from entirely different cultures. The Latin American officers—seven of them, from Argentina, Ecuador, Honduras, Colombia, and Guatemala, all regular army rather than reservists, such as myself—were charming, well-educated, mature professionals, who spoke fluent English. I became particularly fond of Jorge Shaw, an Argentinean captain, and I have always regretted failing to keep in touch with him after the war. To most of us students, including me, war was a temporary shift away from civilian life. But for Jorge and the other Latin American students, the military *was* their life.

My roommate at Sill was a captain I'd met at Roberts. Our barrack was clean and new, but there were all sorts of charges I thought were exorbitant at the time: monthly orderly service for $5 (oh to have that orderly at home, now!), $45 per month for three truly delicious meals a day at the mess—all the steak, ice cream, and watermelon you could eat—and $6 for club dues. Additionally, I responded to artillery school pressure and authorized a pay deduction of $6.25 per month for a defense bond made out to my mother. Even though I was making approximately $200 per month and paying out just $62.25, I still felt that I was being taken advantage of.

My letters show me branching out socially, engaging with more and more diverse groups of friends. I wrote to my parents in early August:

I like and see a lot of the Colorado boys who came from Roberts. I am on good terms with the fellows from Cincinnati. The
rest are from the South, and there is no love lost between us.

But a week later:

We're all getting to know each other better out here and have
picked up several friends among, believe it or not, the boys
from the South. They all say they'd like to come to Calif. and
see the movie stars.

If my prejudice toward the Southern officers had abated, I
cannot say the same for the feelings we generally had about
foreigners. The Germans were "krauts," the Japanese were
"Japs," and this was understandable, even normal, since they
were the enemy. More complicated, though, were our feelings
about our allies—the British in particular. I sent my family a
letter revealing some biases of my own in August 1942:

[I] was told by the instructor in a class on combat intelligence
that all Japs have buck teeth. What a laugh.
    Several F.A. officers arrived back here from observing in
Libya. They say the British army stinks out loud, especially
their officers. They do no maintenance on their materiel, and
let the guns & tanks we send 'em go without oil. They drink
all the time (the officers, that is), and never take the offensive,
but rely on defensive fighting. One captain said the officers
blundered through everything . . . that they "brewed up" morning, noon, and night, etc.

The British army had apparently not been doing at all well
since the war broke out in 1939. But while I was at Fort Sill, a
new commander, General Bernard Montgomery, took charge

of the British forces in North Africa and it soon became a first-class fighting organization.

I had visited England during my European summer tour in 1935 and had always felt warmly about the Brits. So I cannot imagine why I reported the negative views of my fellow officers against our allies across the pond to my very pro-British family. It speaks perhaps to a growing bravado on my part— feigned superiority to mask, perhaps, my continued unease about how a tiny insignificant cog like me was going to fit into this gigantic war machine.

These concerns only worsened when they started to lay on the coursework, which at Fort Sill was demanding to say the least. Our curriculum consisted of an initial two weeks of "Motors" (my nemesis), one week of "Materiel" (equipment and supplies), six weeks of "Gunnery," three of "Tactics," and a thirteenth week of "Communications."

The instructors at Sill were top-notch, teaching with enthusiasm, and definite mastery of their subjects. Some of them, such as Captain Cecil, our portly and respected Gunnery instructor, were warm and personable and took a genuine interest in their students as well. Gunnery, by far the most important subject—if we couldn't shoot, there was no reason for us to stick around—was taught outdoors, with a combination of lectures and working the guns or shooting at targets. If you performed badly in Gunnery, you would be obliged to take the thirteen-week course at Sill all over again. If you did badly during the second go-round, you lost your army commission. It was the only course where such grave consequences prevailed, and so everyone gave the instructors the closest possible attention. I did surprisingly well in Gunnery, ending up in the top tier of my class, which probably gave me the impression that I was more skilled as an artillery officer than I actually was.

The Motors classes, involving the repair and maintenance of everything from gun carts to light tanks, were held in a large garage structure where around thirty students and a variety of mobile equipment occupied every available square inch. The goal of this course was to keep equipment moving, regardless of battlefield conditions. The American army excelled at meeting this goal—a nation of natural-born mechanics, except one fellow named J. R. Boas.

Our Tactics class lectures were indoor affairs, but most of the time the class met outside, reading maps and aerial photos and wandering all over the place. I found that I had a natural ability to read maps, and this ability ended up serving me well in my armored division in combat, where, if you could not read a map, you were blind. Incidentally, and for reasons I cannot explain, this ability to read maps deserted me when I returned to civilian life, and in later years my savior was my GPS.

I found the Communications course to be unbelievably challenging. As I was soon to find out, communicating was the name of the game in armored gun batteries, which were continually on the move. Batteries had to be in constant touch with the fire control center, the forward observer team, the battalion executive officer, the ammunition supply officer, and the medics. Communication was usually by telephone, which meant laying down a lot of wire on the ground. And, when possible, it also included the use of radio transmission. What we had to learn was communication discipline so that everyone would send a message the same way; we were also taught how to acknowledge a message, and what to avoid saying in a message.

Even considering the effort I put in and the reasonable distractions, I could have focused harder on my courses than I did. Though I didn't know it then, I was slated for combat in Europe in 1944 with the Fourth Armored Division, the spearhead of Patton's Third Army, and my role was to be a field artilleryman in support of the division's tanks and infantry. My thirteen weeks at Sill would be crucial to my future performance. I wrote my parents that "75% of the students . . . take the work very seriously and study hard. The other 25% will not wise up until they go into actual battle." It's hard to know which camp I fell into.

Even though I was close to hopeless in Motors, as I consistently failed to correctly troubleshoot the stalled engines presented to us in a classroom exercise, or to perform a 1,000-mile service on a two-and-a-half-ton truck—somehow I managed to squeak by. I wrote home proudly on August 14, 1942:

> I passed Motors, but in the lower brackets, I'm sure. Also passed Materiel (what made you think I didn't?) but in the lower brackets, again. We have had two exams in Gunnery, so far, and I believe that I'm the only one . . . to get a 100 in both. . . . The blasted Southerners, who knew their Motors cold and consequently looked down on me, are sweating in their britches to get through Gunnery—and to a man they all hate it. "He who laughs last."
>
> . . . We start actual firing Monday, & this is the real test. No matter if we know all the rules and mathematics, if we can't hit the target, we flunk. So keep your fingers crossed.

As gunnery was the sine qua non at Sill, success in that particular course was essential. When firing the guns, you had to hit the target within a specified time limit without using more than an allotted amount of ammunition. On our first shoot at Sill, an instructor gave us a target, and for two and a half hours there was nonstop firing—deafening earth-shaking explosions, one after another, over 200 decibels in volume (well beyond the pain threshold). Each shell weighs over fifty pounds, requiring two men to load, and it explodes on impact into a thousand fragments, easily destroying a truck or even a small farmhouse. We must have detonated 200 rounds that afternoon. All of us complained of eyestrain from closely following small, 6 x 6-foot targets and of a ringing noise in our ears caused by the gunfire. Our instructor told us that after the first week of firing our eye and hearing problems would disappear—and he was right. (My hearing began deteriorating about twenty-five years later.)

Successful artillery fire breaks down into two basic components: battery operation and forward observation. Battery operation is all about manning the guns: moving them into position and then loading, aiming, and firing them. The two-and-a-half-ton weapons are mounted on half-tracks with tank treads, which makes them mobile. Since howitzers have a range of many miles, they're typically positioned far behind the front lines, which means the battery operators can't actually see where they're shooting—and that's where forward observation comes in. One officer and a small support team go out in front to find a vantage point where they can see the enemy, track the impact of the artillery shells, and phone or radio back adjustments to help the battery hit the intended targets. That—it turns out—was my forte. The role of the forward observer was crucial, even though he was considered inferior to and of lower rank than the officers who handled the howitzers, doing the actual shooting. The superior status of a battery officer over a forward observer came out in the greater possibilities for career advancement, although the two might start out at equal rank. The battery officer controlled a crew of approximately a hundred enlisted men, whereas the forward observer was on his own with a crew of four or five at most. The battery officer was only at risk when the enemy found his guns and fired at them; the forward observer, on the other hand, was constantly at risk, as he was always close to the enemy. (Not only did I devastate my poor mother by accepting the battlefield over the desk commission, I ended up gravitating toward the most dangerous aspect of field artillery.)

But I couldn't help myself. I enjoyed the challenge of identifying a target's position on a map and calculating the data for our guns, and I got very efficient at it. I learned to score a bull's-eye within two minutes of a new target being assigned, using one minute to calculate and send the data and one minute to allow the guns to fire and the shells to land. Deciding on the target's correct map coordinates was the most difficult task. Calculating distance ("range"), gun angle ("deflection"), and making adjustments when the shots missed the target was known as "indirect fire," an activity I performed until war's end, inflicting considerable damage on the enemy in France, Belgium, Luxembourg, Germany, and, in the last few days of the war, Czechoslovakia. But there the enemy could—and did—shoot back.

As our October 14, 1942, graduation approached, I had no idea where I would be sent next. The army could easily have sent me to the Pacific theater, which would have disappointed me. Hitler, I hated; Hirohito, I didn't really know. But whether they deployed me against Germany or Japan, the army knew there'd be a significant risk of my never returning home.

And so on September 28, 1942, they gave me a standard form to fill out: my will. I left all my assets—about $2,500—to my mother, figuring that she was eighteen years my father's junior and would thus outlive him. (As it turned out, she predeceased him by ninety days.) The will was witnessed by three close friends (two of them from the South!).

# 5

# GOING NOWHERE

**MOST OF MY CLASSMATES AT SILL** went directly to the units in which they would serve for the rest of the war. Not me: when I left the artillery school in October 1942, I was one of the few graduates not yet assigned to a division or battalion. I was simply a field artillery officer on the loose at an army replacement depot (a "repple depple," in army slang), basically killing time for six weeks as I waited to be sent somewhere: the Far East, Europe, or who knew where? Twiddling my thumbs at Fort Bragg in North Carolina was not exactly my idea of a good time. It was demoralizing and disorienting to be stuck in this military oblivion.

My ears were still ringing from all that shooting at Sill. We had fired so many rounds in training (and would continue to do so afterward during the war) that I would develop hearing loss later in life. The army didn't warn us about that—nor did they provide any earplugs. In fact, they did nothing to prepare us for the lifelong toll that we'd endure in going to war. Despite having a good understanding of how the artillery system worked (and a slightly inflated sense of my own skills), I had no knowledge whatsoever of the emotional or psychological effects of what happens to soldiers when we start shooting and killing people. That was not part of the curriculum.

In fairness, I must point out that none of our instructors at Sill had had any combat experience; so they were as ignorant about real war as I was. It had been twenty-two years since our last war. Any field artillerymen still in the service were colonels or generals by now and certainly not doing any instructing; all the other World War I officers had long since retired. So it raises the question: would it have done any good for the army to have found officers who *had* seen combat in 1918–19 and to have them describe to the new generation of World War II officers like me the emotional traumas they might have to endure? My answer: you bet.

To stand close to another human being and gun him down with a pistol, carbine, or rifle and see this human being lying there as a result of your handiwork has a delayed effect on your psyche (it would plague me for a decade). "Post-traumatic stress disorder" hadn't been officially established as a diagnosis, and the idea of telling the troops how to avoid or try to handle depression or the horror caused by what we saw and did in combat was certainly not at the top of the agenda, despite the fact that we were required to attend all kinds of cautionary lectures—many on venereal disease and other unpleasant topics.

There was another noteworthy gap in our Sill education. No one bothered to explain the nuances of how to climb the artillery promotional ladder or how to avoid the career booby trap (where I ended up). We were simply taught to be gun battery officers and shoot the guns, or to find enemy targets and calculate their coordinates as forward observers. What we were never told, however, was that if we became a gun battery officer we would have the opportunity to go from lieutenant to captain, and from captain to major, with a variety of interesting jobs at each level, but that if we became a forward observer we would start as a lieutenant and end as a lieutenant. Forward observing was a promotional dead-end. If there had been a class system in a field artillery battalion, forward observers would have definitely been viewed as second-class citizens. But when it came to dying for one's country, it was the forward observers who led the way.

. . .

In December, after six long weeks of waiting at Fort Bragg, I finally got my marching orders. I couldn't have been happier—I was to join the 65th Armored Field Artillery Battalion, training to fight against General Erwin Rommel, one of the greatest generals in the German army. I felt exhilarated and, frankly, relieved to be going to Europe and not Asia. Well, not Europe exactly. Rommel, known as the "Desert Fox," was deployed in Libya as the commander of Hitler's *Afrika Korps*. The Seventh Panzer Division that Rommel had led in France was one of the most formidable fighting units of the German army, nicknamed the *Gespenster* ("Ghost") Division because of the uncanny speed at which it moved. Speed is everything in armored warfare, and Rommel had been using the impressive mobility of his units to sweep across the Sahara toward Egypt, which was still in British hands. If Egypt fell, the Nazis would control the Suez Canal, a critical supply line to Asia and a major strategic objective—so it was urgent for us to stop him.

To acclimate to North African fighting conditions, the 65th Field Artillery Battalion had been training at the Desert Training Center, a newly acquired army maneuver area in the Mojave Desert of California, which is where I joined them at the end of 1942. I had anticipated being assigned to a division—in those days a unit of about 15,000 men—of which the army was developing hundreds. But my new army orders placed me in a separate, unaffiliated artillery battalion.

I thought of it as an orphan battalion, as it had no connections to a regiment, much less a division. Consisting of about 600 men, the 65th Armored Field Artillery Battalion reported directly to Major General George S. Patton, who had recently been appointed head of the Desert Training Center.

The 65th was commanded by a youngster, Lieutenant Colonel Ed Bailey, who was just twenty-six years old. Merely five years my senior, he was in command of three gun batteries, a headquarters battery, and a service battery. I was twenty-one and in command of nothing: unbelievable! At the rate he was going, he was on track by war's end to become a four-star general.

I admired (and envied) Colonel Bailey. The officers under his command welcomed me with open arms, despite the fact that I was a newcomer and they'd been training as a unit for months. Bailey set the tone—inspiringly nice, as impressive and as pleasant a man as I ever came across in the service. All of his subordinate officers went out of their way to act as hosts, welcoming me as a comrade. I was so happy to be a part of this warm-hearted group of men.

Like many of my companions, I felt this world was where I belonged: the world that was fighting to remove dictators. I knew little about Japan and China and the geopolitical situation in the Far East. But I knew plenty about Hitler and his Nazis; his aggressiveness and territorial ambitions were limitless and guaranteed to continue unless stopped. I belonged in the ranks of those who would attempt to stop him. But this was not to be—at least not yet.

On Christmas Day, 1942, the 65th Field Artillery Battalion got on a train without me, bound for an eastern embarkation port for eventual deployment in North Africa. I was shocked and heartbroken. For reasons I will never know, I had been reassigned to a different division. Maybe it was that I hadn't fully assimilated into the 65th, which had coalesced into such a tight-knit team. Maybe it was simply the fact that other artillery battalions were short of qualified officers. Whatever the reason, it was another blow to my morale and another delay. I had met nothing but friendliness in the 65th battalion: a most unusual experience in the army. They had an air about them that exuded confidence, which is why I hated to see them leave without me. But I had no choice—I had to follow my new orders. Thus, I reported to the 94th Armored Field Artillery Battalion, also stationed at the Desert Training Center. And this unit was a different animal altogether, one that would force me out of my comfort zone.

The 94th was part of the Fourth Armored Division, which consisted of 15,000 men divided into three tank battalions, three infantry battalions, three artillery battalions, plus cavalry, engineers, and the like. My first day with the 94th was anything but auspicious; this new battalion felt like the 65th turned upside down. It began as I reported to the Officer of the Day, Lieutenant G., a disheveled, unthinking type, whose persona screamed "loser." His briefing was haphazard and meaningless. He did offer me a hot coffee (we were in a tent and it was 22 degrees Fahrenheit), but there was something floating in it that looked like a cigarette butt, so I declined his offer.

The tests continued when, on my second night, I was on a field maneuver with a gun battery, and at about 2 a.m. we broke for "lunch." Mine was in a paper bag, a sandwich of sorts: a raw, sliced onion encased in large pieces of hard, stale bread. These minor incidents, a kind of hazing of the new guy, caused my spirits to sink even further. And my mood really plummeted after a humiliating incident on the firing range.

At Fort Sill, the criterion for graduation was the ability to hit the target without wasting ammunition or taking too much time. To do this required getting reasonably close to the mark on one's first shot. In the artillery, the compass circle is divided into 6,400 units called "mils" rather than the traditional 360 degrees. This is done to increase accuracy, with one mil equaling approximately an eighteenth of a degree. It was a metric scale that worked like this: a one-mil shift of the gun would translate into a one-meter correction if your target was 1,000 meters in distance (about 3,300 feet). We calculated our targeting using our calibrated binoculars, compass, and azimuth ruler. In a pinch you could use your finger outstretched at arm's length, which was equal to about 30 mils. You were "reasonably close" if your shot landed within 250 mils (or about three fingers) of its intended target. Anyone whose first shot landed further than 250 mils from the mark became an outcast, or, as they said at Fort Sill, good material for reassignment to the quartermaster corps. In the two and a half months I spent at Sill, I never saw any forward observer make a shift of the guns of more than 250 mils—doing so was unthinkable. Guess what happened to me in the Mojave Desert?

I was out in the field in my jeep (ready with a map, compass, azimuth ruler, binoculars, and radio) to conduct an indirect firing drill. All around me, as far as I could see, was hard sand covered by indistinguishable sagebrush. No hills, mountains, trees, bodies of water, or man-made objects of any sort—only sagebrush. Suddenly, over the radio, came the order to fire on an enemy pillbox at such and such coordinates. The problem for me was locating the position of those coordinates in the desert expanse in front of me.

Of course, I should have kept to Sill's basic cautionary rule to stay within 250 mils when firing the guns; I should have used my map, compass, dividers, and other instruments carefully. Instead, I moved fast, made what I thought was an educated guess, and fired, and as the shell burst far (very far) to the right of what I took to be the target, certainly more than 250 mils, I had no choice but to make a huge (very huge) shift back to the left. Fully aware that I was committing professional suicide, I radioed the guns, "1,000 left," thus vastly exceeding Sill's sacred 250-mil limit, and risking my career as a field artilleryman and my membership in the 94th.

I learned just how badly I was disgraced when, as I was returning to my tent from the latrine that evening, I heard a voice in the officers' club tent ask: "But didn't Boas go to Sill?"

"It is *rumored* he went to Sill," came the reply. This voice belonged to Captain Judson D. Wilcox, the battalion's gunnery officer, a sarcastic and highly critical man who seemed ready to pounce on me from the moment we first met. I returned sheepishly to my quarters. I had thought up to this point that indirect fire was my niche and strength. Now I had screwed up in spades, putting my future as an artilleryman in jeopardy.

. . .

The reveille trumpet sounded in the distance, shaking me from my slumber. I rose groggily to sit up on my bunk and get my bearings. I was living in a pyramidal tent with three other junior officers, all of whom were going through the motions like me of getting prepared to report to duty. But as I stood and reached to pull on my fatigues, Lieutenant Harry Truitt, whose bed was opposite mine, reached for his 45-caliber pistol and growled with dead seriousness: "Lower your pants, Boas!" I hesitated at first, not sure if this was some kind of prank—another hazing routine? But Truitt wasn't kidding around. He cocked his sidearm and hissed: "Don't move!"

I looked down and finally saw why Truitt was so concerned: nestled in the crotch of my fatigues was the largest tarantula I had ever seen, a hairy horror bigger than a hand. When my fatigues hit the ground, Harry—a savior if there ever was one—shot it dead.

Truitt, who hailed from Indiana, proved to be a genial guy. And there were plenty more like him in the 94th. First Lieutenant Bill Walsh was another one I'd met some days earlier at around 2 a.m. on a cold January night when we sat together on a large rock in the desert. Bill was friendly, provided me with some battalion history in a humorous fashion, and assured me that I would fit in well with the 94th's officer corps. He did everything he could to make me feel at home. I made some caustic comments about the onion sandwich I had been served upon my arrival, which brought a smiling response: "When the mess sergeant saw you, he must have figured this is the kind of food you're used to." An ability to insert humor into almost everything was Bill's greatest asset.

Lieutenant G. was shortly transferred out of our division, as was Captain Wilcox; the raw onion sandwich and the 22-degree weather soon became forgotten apparitions of the past. The clincher in getting me accepted in the battalion had been arranged unknowingly by my dear, sweet, not-particularly-successful car-dealer dad, who had loaned me a used car, which would be great for driving to Palm Springs on weekends. The only fellow with a vehicle, I quickly became popular, as everyone wanted to drive with me instead of riding in an army truck.

If ever there were a town that suited the needs of a bunch of dusty and parched artillerymen in need of respite, it was the desert's old, established, and upscale Palm Springs, to which we'd repair at every opportunity. But there was an impediment to these sorties for a person like me. I remember my parents speaking of Palm Springs in pejorative terms, pre-war. "The Desert Inn [Palm Springs' major hotel] is restricted," they'd say, meaning no Jews were allowed to register.

It was the fraternity scene all over again! This time, however, I decided to use the old boy's network to my advantage. I had a college classmate, Owen Coffman, whose family owned the Desert Inn, and I remembered him as being mild and approachable. So I used my Stanford connections and gave Owen a call. When I confronted him on the question of the hotel's policy regarding Jews, Owen assured me that there were no restrictions in place any longer and that all were welcome.

Thus, the Desert Inn hotel became my parents' weekend home away from home, splendid in every respect: gardens, pool, bungalows, ambiance. Occasionally, after spending time with my folks, I'd sneak off to a corner drugstore, where a friendly, beautiful high school girl resided behind the cash register—the daughter of the owners. I wanted to ask her for a date but never could bring myself to do it. In college I hadn't done well with the opposite sex, and my diffidence continued in my early army days.

One of the first officers who rode in my car was none other than my battalion commander, Lieutenant Colonel Alex Graham. Although there was a thirteen-year age gap between us—Graham was thirty-four to my twenty-one—I was never conscious of it because he was so relaxed and friendly, which also served to bridge the big gap in rank between us. But for the fact that he was a lieutenant colonel and I, a lowest-of-the-low second lieutenant, I would have felt like saying, "Let's go get a Coke together."

Graham was so unpretentious that he was a pleasure to have as a passenger. That casualness, however, would turn to laser-focused calm on the battlefield, which made him an excellent leader. I was impressed, among other things, by his appearance. Even donning fatigues and a helmet liner, he was a paragon of neatness. He looked something like how the Prince of Wales had looked when young, but without any foppishness.

In Palm Springs, Graham invited me to a party hosted by his wife, Frances, at a house they were renting while posted in the desert. Frances Graham came from a wealthy family and an impressive military pedigree; born in the Schofield Barracks in Hawaii, she was the daughter of Jacob Devers, who would culminate his career as a four-star general.

When I showed up at their ranch-style home for the cocktail party (they occurred frequently, I soon learned), I saw many other officers from the 94th already there. Frances gave me a warm, smiling welcome and seemed genuinely glad to meet me. She had a natural graciousness that lacked any sign of snootiness or I'm-a-general's-daughter-and-the-wife-of-your-commander-so-you-darn-well-better-be-respectful sort of attitude—quite the opposite. But, to my youthful eyes, she also appeared boisterously loud, rather scantily dressed for a person in her position, and a hard drinker. She handed me a cocktail the moment I walked through the door. Not knowing quite what to do with it, I set the drink down on a nearby table as soon as Frances had turned to another guest. But I soon realized that everyone was drinking.

The parties were really something: high-decibel affairs with men and women shouting to be heard while boozing it up. I felt like an outsider. Almost all the 94th officers were automatically invited, and most were heavy drinkers. Where Frances collected her female guests I do not know, but they were young, loud, and rowdy, wearing short skirts. A few were Hollywood ingenues. One such starlet was Lois Andrews, age eighteen, engaged to George Jessel, a famous comedian in his late fifties. What kind of people did Frances usually associate with? I wondered.

Writing to my mother in February 1943, I grumbled, "The officers in this bn [battalion] (and division, too) have one great fault: they drink like madmen."

Would I ever fit in?

# 6

# DIVISION WITHOUT
# A MISSION

**EVENTUALLY I FIGURED OUT A WAY** to mingle successfully at the Grahams' parties: by pouring myself a glass of sparkling apple juice (on the rocks), which, to outward appearances, might as well have been a whiskey and soda. Over time, my fellow officers welcomed me as part of the team. They were a colorful lot, to say the least.

There was Bill Lothian, a New Yorker who had been an accountant at Pan American Airways; Charlie Gillens, a regular army enlisted man who had risen through the ranks; Tom Cooke, a former hotel night clerk from Atlantic City, New Jersey; John Kelly, the oldest of our group, from New York like Bill Lothian; and finally Bill Walsh, the battalion comedian, whom I had met early on. Each of us played a specific part in the dynamic of our group. Gillens was senior in rank and Kelly was junior, but off-duty no one paid attention to rank. Walsh was the group's humorist, Gillens its militarist, Kelly its senior citizen, Cooke its cynic, Lothian its de facto leader, and I—undeservedly—its academic and intellectual.

Throughout our training and even during the war, Lothian would cook up various weekend scenarios that worked well for our harmonious team of six. Our recreational activities in the Mojave Desert, and later Texas, England, and Paris, produced a natural camaraderie that exceeded anything I have known since. I found these fellow officers friendly, witty, and knowledgeable, and was happy to be accepted by them. Their companionship represented the kind of closeness I had looked for but never found at Stanford. And our friendship only got stronger as time went on. In combat, they were exceedingly brave. In fact, Bill Lothian seemed to thrive in dangerous situations.

There were two things that Lothian appeared to like a lot: Pan American, an employer he worshipped, and explosions. We were once caught in an intense battle in France during which my crew and I were scared stiff, but he was exultant. Bill had led a staid, uneventful life; as an accountant at Pan Am, everything he did was routine, and he therefore relished change, uncertainty, surprise—the very words that describe combat. Lothian got pleasure from anything that broke up the normal routine. Self-confident and relaxed, he was a laconic cynic. I once heard an English girl he was dating say: "Willy, please tell me you love me just a little bit"—to which he replied: "I love you just a little bit."

John Kelly, a second lieutenant like me, was easy to get along with; he seemed content with life and his position in it. The oldest in our group, Kelly married a WAC (Women's Army Corps) second lieutenant who got promoted before he did, and we therefore referred to him as "First Lieutenant Kelly's husband," and, later, as "Captain Kelly's husband," a form of teasing that he definitely did not care for.

The Jersey boy Tom Cooke, a good conversationalist, was curious about everything, despite his cynicism. In fact, he anticipated and laughed at life's downsides and could handle the unpleasant situations that cropped up regularly. He wasn't expecting things to go well and therefore was ready for trouble. It's a quality I wished I had to some degree—for me, every minor setback felt personal somehow, and often devastating. I realized that I stood to learn a lot from men like Cooke.

Charlie Gillens, older than me and superior in rank, went out of his way to treat me nicely (I could do no wrong with Charlie), and, for the life of me, I do not know why. As an enlisted man, Charlie apparently harbored resentments against officers. But he had been savvy and capable enough to qualify for Officer Candidate School (OCS). Although now an officer himself (first lieutenant), Gillens still seemed to nurse some of those resentments.

Tensions between the enlisted men and officers go back to Roman times and the very first structured armies. Most men, whether they're drafted or volunteer, begin their service as lowly privates: foot soldiers on the front lines, or "grunts." If you're any good, you can work your way up to corporal, sergeant, and so on, but there's something of a glass ceiling when it comes to crossing over into the officer corps, unless you're appointed to OCS. Fellows like me who go to Stanford and sign up for ROTC, on the other hand, get a free pass to start their careers as lieutenants, with RHIP and all the other benefits that officer status confers. We are often younger (and certainly less experienced) than the sergeants who report to us, hence the resentment.

Charlie Gillens had been one of those sergeants. Tall, athletic, Irish-handsome with curly dark hair, he was quick with his fists in the enlisted ranks, and he still exhibited a certain pugnacity (but not to me). Charlie got married mid-year in 1943, and his resentments and pugnacity almost disappeared overnight. Gillens knew most of the answers to all the military questions that we rookie junior lieutenants knew nothing about, and he wasn't bashful about sharing his knowledge with the rest of us. So we started calling him "The Swami" after a character on the radio who had absorbed the wisdom of the ages and whose signature phrase was "The Swami knows."

One thing that I learned almost immediately from "The Swami" was the importance of good leadership and a strong chain of command. It's hard to follow someone you don't respect, which is why I was greatly relieved to have as my immediate superior Captain Bob Parker.

Captain Parker, a twenty-six-year-old Harvard grad, had gone to Fort Sill's field artillery school two years before me, studying harder and becoming a good deal more competent. With an uncle who had been a lieutenant general, Parker loved army life; civilian life held no attraction for him at all. (While I, too, wanted to be in the army—it was, after all, my chance to strike down Hitler—once the war was over, I wanted out.) I got to know Parker when I gave him (just like Alex Graham) a ride to Palm Springs one weekend, and we formed what was to become a long-lasting friendship. I liked that he was a blunt speaker who never used subterfuge, that he was interested in the political scene, and that he liked to laugh— so important in the army.

The officers with whom I became close possessed the qualities of humor, mutual respect, constructive attitude, intelligence, and decency. No one had a better balance of these qualities than Parker's boss, Alex Graham, our battalion commander. But he was a deeply private man, seldom expressing his innermost thoughts to anyone. When Graham did communicate, he did so in a direct, firm, soft-voiced manner. In almost three years of observing him daily, I only once heard him raise his voice and lose control. He was a brave man who really knew himself and took the responsibility for our lives and welfare extremely seriously.

Like other officers in the 94th, I quickly came to respect Graham and eventually to almost revere him. I say "almost" because I am not sure if I ever really knew him well enough to know what made him tick. Graham adored being a soldier and seemed to be the happiest of happy campers in his chosen profession, which is probably one of the reasons he married Frances Devers, an army brat if there ever was one. Indeed, everything about Alex Graham—except his quiet, thoughtful unmilitary-like manner—spelled A-R-M-Y.

While we respected and responded to Colonel Graham's understated leadership style, he was something of a rarity among senior officers, most of whom wouldn't hesitate to give you an uncensored piece of their mind. One such man was Lieutenant Colonel Creighton Abrams, an outstanding army tactician who led the 37th Tank Battalion, by far the best in our division. Abrams would end up receiving two Distinguished Service Crosses for heroism in World War II and go on to a stellar military career, as commander of operations in Vietnam and later army chief of staff.

Abrams and Graham had mutual respect for one another and worked well together in combat, greatly increasing the division's combat efficiency. Both were West Pointers who knew what they were doing. Graham treated his officers fairly but firmly in combat; when he gave you an order, it was done calmly. Abrams, on the other hand, could be pretty rough. Tom Cooke, who knew Abrams well, asked him why he spoke so roughly to his tank company commanders. "I want them to be more afraid of me than they are of the enemy," replied Abrams—a comment that leads me directly to our division commander—Major General John S. "Tiger Jack" Wood.

Allow me to set the scene: While our desert training facility had a certain barren beauty with its sagebrush and sporadic Joshua trees, one thing it pointedly lacked—hot running water. We had to take ice-cold showers, or skip them altogether. With elevations up to 5,000 feet, the Mojave is considered high desert, which means nighttime lows in wintertime are routinely subfreezing, but that posed not even the slightest inconvenience to our macho division commander.

In a daily demonstration of his fortitude, General Wood would stand buck-naked in front of his tent every morning and grit his teeth as a pair of orderlies poured helmets of cold water over him, causing him to roar out in shock. If any act ever symbolized toughness and courage, this was it. His exhibitionist ice bucket challenge was meant to inspire us and, oddly, it did. Here was a soldier both gutsy and crazy enough to take on anything; you'd happily follow a man like that into battle. (Ironically, I learned years later at a division reunion long after the war that this ice-cold shower routine was an act—the water had actually been secretly warmed!)

I myself came up with an alternate hygiene strategy while in the subfreezing desert. I learned the trick of keeping clean without showering for months at a time, using only two cups of water: first, brush teeth, but don't rinse; next shave, but don't rinse; next wash body parts, but don't rinse; now cup hands and rinse teeth first followed by face and body parts, in that order. This behavior became so ingrained in me that for many years I continued to rinse using cupped hands after brushing my teeth. Doesn't everybody?

. . .

As the weather warmed, I adapted to the battalion's desert rhythms. I had always wanted to be a captain and a commander of men, and I got a taste of it. As part of "C" Battery, I was ordered to regularly lead the battery's one hundred men in six-mile speed marches, and I found I loved doing it. I learned both desert and celestial navigation easily, and relished the exercise of going, day and night, to remote, unmarked positions in the expanse of the desert. I gave my parents a sense of what it was like:

> We travel at night without lights. I navigate for my battery—
> gosh help me if my calculations are off. I was taught how to
> use the new British desert sun compass at the course and it's
> really lots of fun & makes things very simple. . . .
>
> Yes, we simulate real warfare with everything except live
> ammunition. The umpires make the decisions. Yesterday my
> battery was destroyed by enemy fire.

Losing the simulation hardly dampened my spirits, however. By now, I adored the desert, I liked what I was doing, I had bonded with my colleagues, and, with the car at our service, we had Palm Springs. Life was wonderful, and my letters home reflected almost unlimited enthusiasm.

My superiors must have noticed my growing self-assuredness. I soon found myself reporting to Major Lloyd Powers, who ranked number 2 in the battalion, a pleasant, well-educated, exceedingly proper officer from Chicago. He and I had similar backgrounds and intellectual mind-sets, so we understood and liked each other. Powers, a stickler for rules, which he continually tried to enforce, was too gentle to do so effectively. And he now had a problem on his hands. It seems that some special funds were unaccounted for—around five hundred dollars from the battalion budget. This wasn't a huge amount, but it was enough in those days to make Colonel Graham, the responsible authority, uneasy. No one knew where it had gone, and the man who'd handled the books had been transferred out of the battalion. So Graham ordered an audit, and it was up to Major Powers, his executive officer, to see the order carried out. He picked me—figuring the Stanford guy ought to know his way around a ledger (he was clearly not aware of my less-than-stellar academic record). As luck would have it, I had taken a course in basic accounting the year before, learning about profit and loss statements and balance sheets. So I went to work, and two days later I turned in a report explaining the missing money trail well enough to earn Graham's and Powers's gratitude. "We've seen that if we give you a job you can handle it well," said Powers. "We won't be afraid to use you from now on." Thus, I became the battalion's "Ash and Trash Officer"—basically the battalion's fiscal overseer. Pretty soon my bosses were piling on another extracurricular assignment: lawyering. (Graham and Powers would've had no way of knowing this, of course, but my debate experience at Stanford—where I had to argue both sides of a proposition—made me a pretty decent litigator.) I was definitely excited when they asked me to defend an enlisted man in a special court-martial hearing.

I met the defendant, Private Draper Charles, in the stockade at Mojave. He had been accused of a fairly minor infraction—petty theft, as I recall. I quickly found ways of poking holes in the case against Charles, and—miracle of miracles—I got him off. He was profoundly grateful. Charles eventually became my jeep driver in Europe.

. . .

The Grahams' desert parties continued into the spring, and, feeling more and more part of the team, I allowed myself to try a cocktail or two, discovering it was not an entirely unpleasant experience. I noticed certain men, Lloyd Powers among them, were not shy about two-fisting them back. Yet Alex Graham himself was a teetotaler as was his father-in-law, General Jacob Devers, who attended several of the affairs hosted by his daughter. The triumvirate of Devers, Alex, and Frances was an odd one: from my perspective, both men were quiet, reserved, and made themselves inconspicuous at her parties, while she seemed as noisy and exuberant as could be. It was obvious that Frances and Alex loved one another and that he fully supported her regardless of her antics. I could not fathom what was going on: the Grahams were a social puzzle I did not understand.

Quiet though he might have been at his wife's parties, Graham was undeniably effective as the 94th's commander. His domination of his battalion was total; it would have been unthinkable for anyone in the battalion to have even considered doing something of which he did not approve. It was strange, then, to see Graham, off-duty in Palm Springs (and later in Brownwood, Texas), defer to his revelry-loving wife and lend his full support to her rollicking high-decibel affairs, which often went on until dawn. In a sense there were two Colonel Grahams. In the field he was a fabulous tower of strength, competent, intelligent, brave. But off-duty, unobtrusively passing drinks and hors d'oeuvres to his wife's guests, he seemed to stay behind the lines instead of going out front. The two different faces of Alex Graham perplexed me at the time. I kept asking myself: which one is the real Alex Graham?

I had a hunch that there must be a story behind Frances's behavior, and after the war I found out what it was. In 2008 I learned the story from Dr. Bill Graham, Alex's much younger half-brother, who also went to West Point and eventually became a county coroner in Ohio. He told me that Frances and Alex had been like parents to him. Like her father and husband, Frances loved military life—the only life she had ever known. She was no fool; she had a sound mind and good instincts, coupled with definite qualities of leadership. But Frances had lost her first child in childbirth and found that she was no longer able to have children. Shattered, she began drinking. Bill Graham described Frances as warm-hearted and generous, confirming one of my own early impressions. He added that Frances was much in love with Alex, and he with her, which is why she could do no wrong by him.

There was something touching about their relationship— the loyalty and tenderness between them, despite outward differences. It reminded me, oddly, of my own parents, who seemed deeply connected in spite of the eighteen-year gap in their ages. I wondered: would I ever have a bond like that with a woman? Little did I know, my first taste of it was right around the corner.

. . .

The desert started warming up in mid-March, and the division command began showing our three artillery battalions weekly outdoor movies that started in the early evening. It was at one such movie screening that I came across Dr. Jacob Horowitz. "Doc" (as all of us learned to call him) was on the division artillery staff, but he would become my battalion's medical officer (referred to as the "battalion surgeon") in England and stay on with the 94th through the rest of the war. In his mid-thirties and just five-foot six, he had a prominent nose, a mustache, and a pleasing though quizzical expression, which made me think he looked mouselike.

My relationship with Doc Horowitz turned into a long friendship based on mutual respect. I enjoyed his company in England, admired how he handled himself in combat in France and Belgium, and in a Luxembourg hospital found him playing a rather crucial part in my life by ordering me back to duty in my battalion, overruling the local authorities, who wanted to evacuate me to a hospital back in England.

Pre-war, Doc Horowitz had been a house physician at the Hotel Astor in New York City, where he'd treated a number of celebrities. Doc was not bashful about expressing himself in his booming voice, which could be heard far and wide—a quality quite appropriate for these outdoor movie screenings, where catcalling was part of the fun. This particular evening we were watching a farce starring comedian Ben Blue, and no sooner did the star appear on screen than Horowitz shouted out: "Hey, that's Ben Blue. I cured him of the clap."

This brought the house down with raucous laughter. Venereal disease was something of a touchy subject in the army, which had a habit of showing us graphic and highly unpleasant, even nauseating newsreels about the disfiguring effects of untreated syphilis. I remember one sequence that showed in graphic and dismaying detail what the infection had done to a poor young chap's body. The purpose of these cautionary films was to dissuade soldiers from casual affairs with unknown women. But that was a nonstarter—especially where we were now heading.

The 94th had just been ordered to pack up our base near Palm Springs and proceed to a bivouac in the northern part of the Mojave, Camp Ibis, which had two distinct advantages for us. First, we had a showerhead with hot running water—an unheard-of desert luxury. The other enrichment to our quality of life was proximity to Las Vegas, now within easy driving distance. I'd rate Palm Springs in those days a solid seven, but Las Vegas was a ten plus. Though still in its infancy, we loved Las Vegas for its casual style, the warm hospitality it heaped on the military, and its aura of excitement.

A funny thing happened on my way to Camp Ibis, however—I went AWOL (Absent Without Official Leave), meaning that I was not on duty when I should have been—something any soldier, let alone an officer, is never supposed to be guilty of. I didn't do it intentionally, though. The official time estimate for the move from Palm Springs to our new desert camp near Needles in California (packing up tents, supplies, equipment, weaponry, etc.) was three to four days. I was told to drive my car straight through to the new location and await the battalion's arrival there, but, figuring I had days to spare, I detoured through Las Vegas.

It would be a few more years before Bugsy Siegel and the mob swept into town and developed the strip, but Vegas still had a couple of decent establishments with gambling, women, and entertainment. The choices boiled down to El

Rancho Vegas and The Last Frontier. El Rancho, a glorified motel, was pure charm and fun; The Last Frontier, a small precursor of the garish Las Vegas hostelries to come, dwarfed El Rancho, though it was certainly not as quaint. El Rancho had a perfect-size pool, not too large or small and aesthetically designed. There was a loggia-style patio used for dancing at night and plenty of women available as dance partners.

I tried my hand at blackjack for modest amounts and not for too long, but I was fascinated watching a fellow lieutenant play for hours on end and lose consistently. Each time he lost, the croupier would intone, "Too bad, Lieutenant," a phrase I began to use thereafter whenever a friend had a problem. And as he lost and lost, the lieutenant would constantly hit the table with his fist and demand of the croupier: "Goddamn it! How come you always win?" To which the croupier's standard answer was: "Beats the shit out of me, Lieutenant"—a phrase so catchy, I still use it to this day.

After my Las Vegas detour, when I finally reached Camp Ibis, I realized to my chagrin that the battalion was already firmly ensconced (having arrived a day early), which meant I was officially AWOL. Major Powers told me I was to be confined to camp for a month—meaning no weekend leaves. But he said so with a smile rather than a scowl. I feel I was treated exceptionally well under the circumstances, probably because I'd earned my stripes earlier in the battalion audit. Still, it was no fun having to stay behind while all my pals went gallivanting off to Las Vegas, and I said as much in a letter home.

My kind-hearted dad (who at this time was sixty-seven) came to visit and keep me company while I was confined to camp. I was touched by his companionship, but after a day or so I told him to take off with the guys, who had planned a weekend in Las Vegas. He ended acting as a kind of host for five or six of my closest officer friends (Bob Parker and Tom Cooke among them) at the El Rancho hotel, while I remained behind. Apparently, my father was a great success with them, as he had been, previously, with my college friends. When at dinner Parker needed a dance partner, my dad asked him whom he admired among the young ladies present across the dining room floor—and off he went to broker the encounter, by politely asking the one Bob had pointed out if she would care to dance with the handsome captain across the room. The answer was yes.

One of the reasons that there seemed to be an abundance of apparently single females in Vegas was that Nevada was a no-fault divorce state, the only requirement being six weeks of residency in the state. Thus, a number of women were living at El Rancho for extended stays while securing their divorces, and I was lucky enough to make the acquaintance of one of them.

Buoyed by the success of my fellow officers, I got up the nerve one night to approach a lovely lady named Billie Brandt. In her early thirties, Billie was considerably older than me, but I didn't even realize it at first. She just seemed extremely kind and very pretty. Dancing led to drinks, and then—well, Billie became my first real girlfriend. (I had had a few flings at Stanford, but nothing lasting.) Billie seemed to really care for me (I found out later that she thought I was the nicest young man she'd ever met).

As we began dating, I learned that Billie had been married to an air force major, with whom she had a three-year-old daughter, who was with her. I didn't probe about the circumstances of their breakup; I didn't think it was particularly my business. But certainly Billie had a lot more life experience than I did. Here I was just twenty-two—she, ten years my senior and a mother. Yet none of that mattered to me. Billie was a lovely, well-mannered person, a lady in every respect, and we liked one another a lot. We both thought during the weeks we saw each other in Nevada that the relationship might endure. But that, sadly, didn't come to pass for reasons that were bigger than both of us.

. . .

On May 12, 1943, General Erwin Rommel raised the white flag and surrendered his decimated Afrika Korps to the Allies. It was a stunning reversal of fortune for Germany. Earlier in the North African campaign, Rommel had used his signature blitzkrieg ("lightning war") tactics to devastate the British forces and push them deep into Egypt to the east. But then the Americans entered the fight from the west, in Morocco and Tunisia, under the command of General Dwight D. Eisenhower, and later George Patton, both of whom had served, like Rommel, as tank commanders in World War I. Since late 1942, the British and American armies in Africa had been squeezing the German forces from both sides and cutting off their supply lines; yet Hitler refused to allow Rommel to retreat and regroup.

Reduced to just twenty working tanks by the spring of 1943, Rommel had no choice but to surrender the Afrika Korps, which meant some 275,000 German soldiers became Allied prisoners of war. Rommel himself retreated to Greece, then eventually back to Germany. But Hitler never fully trusted Rommel, despite his brilliance as a military strategist. One reason for this was that Rommel's popularity in Germany had predated "Der Führer"—he'd been a hero in World War I, long before Hitler's rise to power. And Rommel did not share Hitler's anti-Semitic views, refusing to have any part in the extermination of Jews. Ultimately, Rommel became implicated in a plot to overthrow the Führer, and Hitler gave him a choice: face a military tribunal (with the threat of disgrace and severe reprisals to his family and loyal staff) or commit suicide. Rommel, dignified to the bitter end, swallowed the cyanide pill.

Germany's withdrawal from North Africa changed the whole ball game for the Fourth Armored Division. We'd been training for months for desert warfare, with its open terrain and punishing conditions. Now it was anyone's guess where we'd be deployed.

The army brass figured out one thing quickly enough: no point in keeping us isolated out here in the Mojave Desert, which was remote and hard to supply. We were ordered to move, once again, to Camp Bowie in Texas, which meant my nascent romance with Billie Brandt was about to be geographically challenged (in fact, we would end up falling completely out of touch).

The combined setbacks—the loss of our mission and my parting ways with Billie—took a toll on me. Writing home to my grandmother on May 17, I unburdened myself to her concerning my crumbling state of mind:

> A person sometimes gets a lot of stuff stored up
> inside of himself, which he has to mentally get rid of.
> I'm afraid I was and still am in that stage when I . . .
> will not feel sure of myself. . . . I'm sure that by the
> time we get set to do our part in this affair that I'll be

a man with a sound and clear-thinking mind. Hope I'm not mistaken.

But deployment into battle was not even on the horizon at this point: the Fourth Armored was now a division without a mission. Where on earth would they end up sending us?

"Beats the shit out of me, Lieutenant."

My grandmother Annie Kline, my mother, Larie, and my father, Benjamin, in 1942. When I started my officers' training at Camp Roberts, they would drive south some 200 miles from San Francisco to visit.

Later, when I was stationed in the Mojave Desert, my parents and grandmother traveled some 420 miles to visit, spending weekends in nearby Palm Springs.

Holding my trusty binoculars in the front row of my Battery Officers Class #65 at Fort Sill, Oklahoma, in 1942. All field artillery officers had to undergo special training, learning how to locate the enemy and operate the guns.

Behind a battery commander's telescope at Fort Sill. Proficiency with this instrument is a first step in spotting and calculating the whereabouts of enemy fire.

Practicing at Fort Sill
with the aiming circle,
an instrument used to
establish map coordinates
for the battery's guns.

My favorite Fort Sill
instructor, Captain Cecil,
who was not only very
precise in his teaching of
Gunnery but also showed
a personal interest in his
students.

With the boys from Colorado at Fort Bragg on Thanksgiving Day in 1942: (from left) Lieutenants Ken Grush, Don Walt, me, Ken Cline, and Paul Desjardins. We had first met during a ROTC exercise at Camp Ord in 1941 and then undergone training together at Camp Roberts and Fort Sill. We became good friends, and I regret not keeping up with them.

At mess in the field at Fort Bragg, North Carolina, in 1942. I was just marking time at this "repple depple" (replacement depot), waiting for a full-time assignment.

On the phone at the rifle range at Fort Bragg, monitoring my fellow officers' marksmanship.

# 7

# I ASK FOR A FLASK

**I DON'T WANT TO MINCE WORDS.** Camp Bowie, located outside the town of Brownwood in the heart of Texas, was totally humdrum. I know this because, for the life of me, I can't remember a thing about it. I've always retained vivid recollections of what Roberts, Sill, and our two base camps in the desert looked like, but Bowie draws a blank.

The Fourth Armored Division was playing the waiting game at Bowie, basically inactive while standing by for orders as to where it would go next. And there was a huge logistical hurdle we were tasked with—to cut our manpower from 15,000 to 10,000 men, which meant one-third of us (and quite possibly me) would be in military limbo. The rationale was that by streamlining our ranks we'd be leaner and meaner and therefore more efficient in battle. But it was an administrative monster to reorganize a division like this. And, in a virtual repeat of my disastrous 1,000-mil gun shift in the

Mojave Desert, I, once again, did myself no career favors in Texas. The lesson this time involved internal politics.

It began, as these things often do, with a sudden uptick in fortune. On July 13, 1943, I became a battery executive officer, second in command of one hundred men and responsible for the performance of six 105mm howitzers, eleven percent of the division's total artillery firepower. I was surprised and thrilled by the assignment. It's every Fort Sill graduate's dream to be a battery executive, because, if you are any good at it, it leads to the job of battery commander and a captaincy. Up to this point, my focus had been as a forward observer, out in front and all alone. Now I'd be back with the guns and interacting with the men. Over the moon, I wrote to my mother on July 15:

> By some let-up of ill fate I've had the good fortune to land the executive officer's job in "A" Battery. It's something I've waited a long time for and I'm really delighted. The battery has a new commander (the ex-exec) so it'll be tough sledding until I've learned the ropes. . . . Now I'll be working the guns instead of out in front observing.

The eighteen howitzers belonging to the 94th Field Artillery Battalion were divided into three batteries, designated "A," "B," and "C." Up to this point, I had been serving in "C" Battery under Bob Parker, now commanded by Bill Lothian, the thrill-seeking former number-cruncher from Pan Am. "B" Battery was led by another friend—(battalion funnyman) Bill Walsh. Had I been assigned to report to either of the Bills, with whom I got along famously, I would have felt right at home. But, as luck would have it, I got "A" Battery, where I had no relationship whatsoever with my new boss, Lieutenant

Morris (Ralph M.) Click, an inexperienced battery commander who had just moved up from the executive position himself. My discomfort was compounded by not knowing any of the battery's NCOs (noncommissioned officers) either, especially its first sergeant, James Flinchum. Politically speaking (not that the army is supposed to be political), first sergeants were crucial in getting you "accepted" by the battery's enlisted ranks. My letters home begin to suggest the challenges I was now facing:

> Since taking over my new job, find the going pretty rough. The men have been used to their old officers (who were good ones) for a long time . . . they've probably got my number (whatever it may be) doped out by this time. They're such a darn fine bunch—real honest-to-God men, they deserve better leadership than what I'll be able to give them.

I felt like an odd man out with Lieutenant Click and A's first sergeant, Flinchum; it seemed, from the day I arrived, that I was trespassing and not in step (I was obviously not a trespasser, as I was there under orders, but I certainly felt out-of-sync with the rest of the team, a condition that turned out to undo me). At the beginning of August, things looked up for a moment and I wrote:

> The new job is smoothing out, after considerable initial difficulties. It's the best job in the army, so am doing my damndest to hold on to it. . . . I know I can stand another month in the battery before I'll start to click.

But the fact is, I never "clicked" with Lieutenant Click. I cannot recall ever having a real conversation with him, other than an occasional automatic "hello." Even though we served together in the battalion, saw one another daily, attended the same mess, played in the same poker games, and shared whatever social life there was in an officer corps of thirty members, we never had any kind of real relationship. This did not bode well. Military units must be tight-knit in order to function efficiently under the crucible of battle. I certainly was feeling the heat in August, when I wrote my father:

> I have never worked harder or more earnestly than I have the past month. However, have run into a lot of trouble & setbacks and received some big disappointments recently. Won't bother you with the gory details—hope things will work out o.k. someday. Life is kind of miserable at the present and, frankly, I'm worn out.

On August 13, just a month after my appointment, I was kicked out of "A" Battery. Immediately, I began to berate myself, thinking of all the ways I could have played things differently. Why hadn't I gone higher up in the system when things began to unravel to ask for advice? I certainly could have approached Captain Parker, who had ridden in my car numerous times and who was a few years older and wiser. He probably would have told me the lesson of the day: if there's friction with your boss, don't stand on ceremony—start massaging his ego. And don't go into a job unprepared. I had been concentrating on indirect firing as an observer while I should have been boning up on battery management and howitzer technique.

Losing such a desirable job after only a month was a knockout blow, and I never really got over it, despite the distractions available to me. My attitude toward the Grahams' cocktail parties, hosted by Frances at their new house in Brownwood, changed. This time when she handed me a drink I held onto it.

One piece of good news was that Charlie Gillens, the former sergeant turned lieutenant, got married while we were in Texas, to a charming schoolteacher from Massachusetts named Mary. They shared a house in Brownwood with Bill and Annette Walsh, and I was invited there for Sunday night dinners. My warm and friendly hosts made me feel at home, and their presence in this house provided the only acceptable environment I found while at Camp Bowie.

Charlie's best man when he married Mary was Tom Cooke. I had become friendly with Charlie and Tom in the desert, and these friendships solidified in Brownwood. One of the things that I liked best about Charlie was his steadfast character. Later, when we were in England, he impressed me by the contrast with some other married officers, who took up with lonely English women whose husbands were serving abroad. Charlie, one of the best-looking men in the 94th, stayed totally aloof and faithful to his new wife. He stood tall.

I was fortunate to still have my car with me in Brownwood—one of the very few to have such a luxury—and it made weekend touring easy. Tom Cooke and I met girls in Dallas, often having to choose when we met a twosome—once, actually, a mother and a daughter—as to who would escort whom. Tom, who had clerked in a hotel as a civilian, was a consummate diplomat, and thanks to him we always seemed to agree. This mild gallivanting around together in Texas buoyed my spirits somewhat.

A far less auspicious memory I have of my time at Camp Bowie concerns the inexplicably shabby way I treated my mother when she wrote asking to come visit me. We had always been close, and she wanted to come to Texas to see me after visiting a friend of hers in Mexico. I forbade her to do so, writing: "Now, this is *important!* Do not come to Texas." The visit would have meant a lot to her, and I know she must have been hurt by my rejection. If it had been my dad, Ben Boas, or my maternal grandmother, Annie Kline, I would have said, "Great! Come on." There was something about my mother's proposed visit that scared me, and, spineless, I let fear take over. What was it exactly?

Fear of her as a brilliant intellectual amid a battalion largely devoid of that kind of culture; fear that her strong sense of humor, often based on criticizing others, might offend; fear that, although she was very well mannered, she might be difficult if crossed? I guess it boiled down to this: I was afraid she would embarrass me with her outspoken and critical opinions. And so instead of saying, "Love to see you, Mom," I turned her down, and have been ashamed of myself ever since for this slight.

The army has a way of applying its own kind of therapy. Not long after this episode with my mother, I was dispatched for one month to Louisiana, to serve as an artillery umpire in an army maneuver. It was during this time that a crucial incident occurred. After thirty days in the Louisiana backcountry, I had a weekend in New Orleans, and a lovely girl I met guided me around a city jam-packed with military. She had told me about a candy I had never heard of before—pralines—and she easily found a shop that sold them. I bought pralines for my parents and grandmother, paid, and left the shop. And then, suddenly, the thought occurred to me: I should send some to Frances Graham in Brownwood. Why this particular inspiration came to me, I never knew. There was nothing I wanted from

Frances or Alex. I was a discharged battery executive officer, and I knew there was no possibility of getting my job back. It was simply that I liked them a lot, and that sending them the pralines along with a nice card in the box was a way to express this feeling. So back into the store we went. The card was written and the box of pralines purchased and sent. And all I can say about this decision is: Boy! What timing!

As the Fourth Armored Division scaled back from 15,000 officers and men to 10,000, the officer corps of the 94th would be cut from forty-five to thirty. My good friend Bill Sovacool, like me a recently failed battery exec transferred back to being a forward observer, was out. The 94th's liaison officer (the top staff job in the battalion) was out, and that job went to Tom Cooke as a promotion. Tom had been the battalion adjutant, an important staff job that ranked just below that of liaison officer, and the adjutant's job went to—hold on—me!

I never learned if Frances put in a good word for me upon receiving the box of pralines. Was it God and my Christian Science prayers that brought about this turnaround? Was it the pralines that convinced Colonel Graham both to keep and promote me (the adjutant's job called for a captaincy, although that, strangely, never came through)? I will never know, but I am pretty certain those candies didn't hurt.

My appointment sent a message throughout the battalion that Colonel Graham had confidence in me. The fact that my captain's bars were never received (the army brass pushed promotions for line officers but *not* for staff ones) didn't bother me at the time, since I knew that I was, in fact, serving in a captain's role.

Then, two weeks after getting this new assignment, came an exciting surprise: we were ordered to pack up and move to

Taunton, Massachusetts, and thence to Boston for shipment overseas. I made out another will, filled out forms sending most of my salary to a bank back home, and asked a Dallas businessman I'd been introduced to by a friend of my family to sell my car, telling him whatever he got for it was fine (it was my father's car and I was being cavalier about it). I wrote my dad on December 1, 1943:

> Our destination is [a] mystery, but . . . the consensus . . . is England. . . . Everyone is looking forward to the fray. . . . [I] should be able to take care of myself. I am not worried . . . although I don't know exactly what sort of an account I will give of myself. . . .
>
> P.S. You asked me what I could use for Xmas, Dad, and, frankly, I'd like a flask. . . . Thought perhaps I could use yours.

A non-drinker no more, I knew that having my dad's flask meant that whiskey would always be available.

Once the orders came sending the Fourth Armored Division overseas, we were given two weeks to store our garrison paraphernalia, pack up the rest, and get ready to depart. My parents and grandmother came from San Francisco to New York City to say good-bye and arranged to give me a dinner party with a lot of their friends at the Savoy Plaza Hotel. I came down from Taunton to be with them. My father brought his flask; my mother kept her tears in check. And next thing I knew I was boarding a ship for Europe.

The memory of this moment remains etched in my mind in vivid detail: marching up the gangway of our troopship on Christmas Eve, my dad's silver flask in my coat pocket, cheered on by a bevy of young Red Cross women who were positioned at the foot of the gangway, giving us cookies, doughnuts, candy, and pleasant banter. As they smiled and waved, we called out, "Will you be my New Year's Eve date?" and, more boldly, "Will you remain faithful to me until I get back?"

They answered: "Of course—yes—delighted to!"—and so forth.

It was a rite as old as civilization itself—young soldiers marching off to war, still innocent, not knowing the trials they will face as the girls cheer them on, clinging to the hope that their champions will prevail and vanquish the enemy. But there was an unspoken tension underlying this spirited pageant—the elephant in the room that caused some of the young women to avert their eyes and brush away a tear.

One in five of us would die in battle.

# 8

# DON'T COMPLAIN
# ABOUT WARM BEER

**THE LAST TIME I HAD SAILED** across the Atlantic, in 1935, the circumstances were vastly different. I was a thirteen-year-old boy on a luxury ocean liner surrounded by a trio of doting women—my mother, great-aunt, and grandmother, who had picked up the tab for our European trip. My grandmother, Annie Klein (later, Kline), inherited wealth from her late husband, Sigmund, who had made his fortune manufacturing and selling whiskey before dying young. Annie had offered the free trip to my dad as well—but, not wanting to be surrounded by women for an extended period of time, he opted to stay home. Based on my own experience as the only male who *did* go on the trip, I would say Dad showed good judgment. Now, in 1943, I found myself in the opposite situation: one of 10,000 men, with ne'er a woman to be seen. And this wasn't exactly an ocean liner.

Well, actually, it was. We shipped out on the *Santa Paula*, a converted Grace Line luxury cruise ship on which my parents had been passengers fourteen years earlier, on a trip through the Panama Canal. With millions of soldiers to ship overseas, the U.S. Army was commandeering every seaworthy ship it could get its hands on. It had stripped these vessels down to their bare essentials to be able to cram as many bodies (and armaments) on board as they could, which made for quite a contrast to my former experience.

Transatlantic travel on the *SS Washington* back in 1935 had been sublime, with our every possible want catered to: gourmet dining, solicitous stewards, movies, a dance orchestra, a swimming pool, and spacious public areas. First-class passengers even brought along their valets and maids. The voyage from New York to Southampton took just five speedy days.

Troopship travel in December 1943 on the converted *Santa Paula* was another matter: ten of us second lieutenants were in a room meant for two, and we ate decidedly non-gourmet chow in half-hour shifts in the officers' mess. Instead of stewards, we had navy mess attendants who were referred to as "number one boy, number two boy," and so forth; instead of swimming in a pool, we had continual lifeboat drills; instead of a zippy five days at sea, it took our convoy, weighted down with machinery and troops, eleven; instead of dances, we had seasickness and boredom; instead of movies, we got lectures on how to behave in England, prompted by Eisenhower's desire to avoid unnecessary clashes between American forces and the British. The good-behavior-in-England lectures were not only timely but downright amusing. "Do not complain about warm beer" was one injunction. Another: "Do not walk on the grass." And, critically important: "Remember that sus-penders are called braces."

In addition to the 10,000 men, a new element had crept aboard the ship, one that was not with us in the United States: fear. The unforeseen disappearance of our sergeant major on the gangway at Boston may have introduced it. Just moments before our departure, the battalion's highest-ranking NCO, a professional soldier no less, had gone AWOL (which, at this juncture, was a capital offense, we were told). I never found out what happened to him, but I certainly realized—we all did—that if someone as outstanding as the sergeant major had gone AWOL out of fear, we were all heading into serious danger.

I had been in the army eighteen months, and do not recall any training, or even discussions, on how to manage fear in combat. For most of the troops, myself included, the antidote was either not to think about the consequences of battle or to adopt the fantasy: "It won't be me." Another antidote was drink, of which I now partook with regularity. Also there was nightly poker, with its natural companion: bravado. No big surprise here; macho posturing is guaranteed to occur any place where rowdy men are confined in close quarters.

Indeed, it seemed to be gung-ho exuberance that drove the *Santa Paula* to its dock in Swansea, Wales, at 1 a.m. in ear-ly January 1944. Our disembarkation in total darkness was full of ribald songs and insulting exchanges with our British hosts, Eisenhower's behavioral lectures notwithstanding. The British seemed genuinely pleased to have us, but we were not so generous in return. A common volley:

"Glad to have you, Yanks!"

"You damn well ought to be, you limey so-and-so!"

We had arrived under the cover of darkness and our exact location in England was top secret. We could not discuss it in letters home, or with anyone for that matter. Control of information is absolutely critical during wartime. When important plans fall into enemy hands, it can be disastrous.

Just nine months prior, the Allies had suffered a terrible blow to this effect. In April 1943 a Spanish fisherman recovered the body of Major William Martin, a pilot with the British Royal Marines, who had washed ashore on the beach at Punta Umbria, presumably after having ejected unsuccessfully from his aircraft. The dead pilot had an attaché case handcuffed to his wrist, so it was clearly of high value. The fisherman turned over the corpse to the German authorities, ensconced in Spain through their alliance with Spanish dictator Francisco Franco (the Nazis also controlled the rest of mainland Europe at this point).

German intelligence agents pried open the locked briefcase to discover a trove of highly classified documents (along with love letters from Martin's fiancée). These included detailed plans of the next move for the Allied forces, which had just triumphed in North Africa and were now looking for a way to cross the Mediterranean and establish a beachhead in southern Europe.

Attempting to move an army across a body of water is a laborious and precarious proposition, which is why these plans were so secret. We would need to airlift a certain number of troops in hopes of parachuting them behind enemy lines (very risky), and we'd also be attempting an amphibious invasion—even riskier, because the Nazis had been steadily fortifying every inch of coastline. To make matters worse, they now knew (from the recovered documents) exactly where we were planning to invade: Sardinia and Greece.

But there's a twist to this story. It was a *lie*—an elaborate and brilliant deception by British counterintelligence. "Major Martin" was actually a homeless man from Wales who had committed suicide; the plans and the love letters (even the picture of his fiancée!) were all fabrications, intended to throw off the Nazis from our real objective: to invade Sicily. It worked like a charm. The bogus documents were rushed back to Berlin, where Hitler bought them hook, line, and sinker. We knew this because, fortuitously, we had recently cracked the Nazis' Enigma code and could intercept Hitler's communications ordering reinforcements to Sardinia and Greece—even while his Italian ally, Benito Mussolini, vehemently disagreed, arguing that Sicily, only a hundred miles from Tunisia, must surely be the real target. But Mussolini was clearly second banana, and Hitler's decision prevailed, which allowed the Allied forces, led by U.S. General George Patton and British General Bernard Montgomery, to take Sicily.

By early 1944 our troops were halfway up the Italian peninsula, and we now needed to establish a second front in France. We were faced, once again, with the same predicament—how to move a massive army across a body of water (in this case, the English Channel). To defend against such an attack, Hitler brought in (who else?) his best commander, Erwin Rommel, now field marshal (and still in Der Führer's good graces). For months now, Rommel had been overseeing a series of impressive fortifications, dubbed the "Atlantic Wall," along 2,400 miles of coastline from Norway to Spain. Reinforced concrete pillboxes (to house machine guns and anti-tank artillery) were built at regular intervals along the bluffs, and over six million mines were scattered across the beaches. There were underwater mines, too, to prevent ships from even landing. The most colorful of the defensive measures were the *Rommelspargel* ("Rommel's asparagus"): slanted poles peppered across open areas with sharpened tips, designed to impale parachutists and gliders.

As the Germans fortified their Atlantic Wall, the Allies were simultaneously devising plans for D-Day, which would take months of coordination. Much like the invasion of Sicily, it would involve an elaborate red-herring operation (commanded by none other than Rommel's archrival, General George Patton).

Of course, at the time, none of this bird's-eye view was visible on the ground by me, a lowly lieutenant. I simply knew that we were playing another waiting game in England, as we had at Fort Bragg, in the Mojave Desert, and in Texas. But I wasn't at all disheartened this time, for I was finally in Europe, within a stone's throw of the action. I described my first impressions of England in detail to my family on January 16, 1944:

> We're now in England, exact location a secret. The weather has been . . . terrifically foggy. It's hard to see 10 yds ahead of you in the daytime and navigation in the night blackout is some problem. The blackouts in [England] are total—not a light shows. When we go to town, we grope our way around. Mother—you wouldn't recognize England—they've really been through hell and the squeeze on all people, particularly the middle class, is really rough. The women, more than anyone else, have certainly passed through a metamorphosis . . . they

lack soap, cosmetics, soft clothes (i.e. silk, etc.), the hands of the gals are all coarsened and hardened.

We would end up staying in England for almost eight months, spending most of our time living in the Prince Maurice Barracks, a borrowed British facility located outside of the small, medieval market town of Devizes, a part of Wiltshire that we got to know well. What appealed to me most about Devizes was its old-world charm. Every aspect of this ancient hamlet was inviting: its aesthetic town square dating to the Middle Ages; its two hotels, each with pleasing public rooms in which to dine or drink; its cinema, where before the film began the audience would rise and sing "God Save the King" with emotion. I even recall being impressed by its hardware store, to which I recall going quite often—I'm not sure whether to buy things or to see and try to talk to the pretty but standoffish girl behind the counter. Still shy alone, I did better with a wingman. Here's how I reported my first overnight excursion:

> Spent last night in . . . Devizes—near Bath. Took a room at the old Bear Hotel and then Woody [Lieutenant Darrell Wood] and I did the town—meaning we took a couple of limey broads to a movie, a pub, and home. Then we had a couple of shots of brandy from Dad's flask (gosh I'm glad I have it) in the hotel lounge by the fire, and so to bed. The hotel was lovely, reeking with respectability and age. ("You know, gentlemen, we don't allow lydies in the rooms.")

One of the perks for Americans in Devizes was the plethora of attractive, marriageable, middle-class young women to be met and wooed. This meeting and wooing usually took place at dances held in the town hall, with a small live band, plenty of soda, and (warm) beer. The local girls seemed to prefer our enlisted men as dates, but when we first arrived in Devizes, we were told that they would only make love if the lovemaking was done standing up. (This position would, supposedly, keep pregnancy at bay; as far as I know, this concept was believed and followed by one and all.)

To us young bachelor officers, it did not seem unusual that some of our married senior colleagues found girlfriends in England; being overseas, in our minds, created new standards. But there certainly was resentment among many British servicemen toward their American counterparts who were dating English women, summed up succinctly with the oft-repeated Q&A: "What are the three things wrong with the Americans?" "They're overpaid, oversexed, and over here."

Some of the officers got very serious about the women they encountered. Second lieutenants Darrell Wood and Don Guild both met enchanting young women at the dances and married them in Devizes shortly thereafter. The father of Darrell's bride was a British army colonel fighting in Italy, so she was given away by Colonel Graham at a lovely wedding that we all attended. The life of the party was my old pal Bill Walsh, who had gotten hold of some booze earlier in the day and who was, by dinner, completely sozzled. He cheerfully insulted everyone present, including our understated commander, Colonel Graham, whom Walsh mocked with a pitch-perfect impression. He even made fun of our British hosts—impeccably good sports, they roared with laughter. There was only one problem with his speech. Walsh was an impossible act to follow and guess who was slated to speak next: Lieutenant J. R. Boas.

I rose nervously, cleared my throat, and unfolded the toast I had written down on a scrap of paper, fumbled for my glasses, cleaned them with my handkerchief and put them on, before smiling nervously at the crowd. And that's when Walsh gave out a wolf cry from across the room, yelling: "Old wolf Boas is looking 'em over again. Give him a big smile, girls." It brought down the house. Again.

. . .

With the dances and general merriment during our stay in Britain, we almost forgot sometimes we were at war. On a weekend visit to the port of Bristol, that reality came crashing back to me. The city was a man-made disaster zone. Bombed beyond recognition by the Luftwaffe during the Battle of Britain, it was a lifeless expanse of misery that totally erased the exuberance I'd been associating with being in England. Seeing the effects of war up-close was far different from reading about it in a book. As I gazed out across the indiscriminate destruction, I felt a paroxysm of fear surge in my belly, and it hit me: I'd soon be in the war up to my neck.

Fortunately, we were doing everything we could to be prepared for it. The division brass saw to it that our firing exercises never ceased, although we were considered well trained after months and months of work in the desert and Texas. Nonetheless, we improved our skills further with firing practice on the Salisbury Plain. The plain, a 300-square-mile training area in Wiltshire belonging to the UK's defense department, was twenty-five miles south of our camp in Devizes and a great place to practice gunnery, as it was uninhabited and there were almost no nearby towns.

One day, during our firing exercises, I was waiting my turn to step into my role as a forward observer and practice estimating the firing coordinates for our designated target. I happened to be preceded on this morning by a junior lieutenant who let his nerves get the best of him, not only missing the target by a mile but manhandling the battery commander's scope so severely as to render it useless.

"Have that officer stand down!" boomed the harsh voice of Colonel Ernest Bixby, our no-nonsense division artillery commander, and the poor chap, shaking and disgraced, removed himself.

I was next. I steeled myself and surveyed the target—a towed wooden vehicle. As the scope was now useless, I just guessed at the coordinates. Somehow through sheer luck— it could not have been anything else—the shot was a direct hit and destroyed the target. There must have been close to a hundred field artillery officers at this firing exercise, and there was dead silence—I couldn't hear a sound. And then, once again, Bixby's voice. "That's what I call shooting!" it crowed.

In an instant I was redeemed. My bull's-eye on Salisbury Plain had completely erased my reputation as an unpardonable shooter, held over from my mistake in the Mojave Desert. Suddenly, after more than a year in professional oblivion, I was rehabilitated, and everyone's attitude toward me changed. That night at dinner my tablemates were super-courteous: "More coffee, Boas?" "Can I pass you the cookies, Boas?"

. . .

One of the greatest bonuses of our long deployment in England was the chance to spend weekends in London, but they did not come cheaply. I was outraged, for example, that a first-run movie in London cost as much as $2.50, compared to about half that in the U.S.—and that was without a double-feature, which was standard in America. I communicated my financial woes to my family, especially my father (who was having his own share of serious business problems as his small Pontiac dealership had no Pontiacs because the factory in Michigan was only making military vehicles). In one letter I complained:

> Financially am quite flat so my social life will be pretty nil in the future. As I send $82 to the bank, $37.50 for a war bond, $6.50 for insurance, leaves about $60.00—of that $60.00, $18.75 goes for food, $9.00 for laundry (very high over here), $8.00 per month for fees to pay for our Sat. nite dances— leaves [less than] $30.00. Then—after buying the paper— getting Woody a present, etc., I haven't much left. My leave used up the Express checks—and I went to London last Sunday on poker winnings—but took a beating last nite so I'm back where I started. What the hell! Incidentally, we can't receive money from home without getting the C.O.'s [Colonel Graham's] permission—so this is not to be construed as a touch.

But it certainly was a touch, and my kind and generous dad cabled me some money. I was twenty-two and surely didn't need to write to my father in a twelve-year-old fashion. Nor did I need to be such a London spendthrift. An only child, I was long used to my parents' thoughtful but not lavish support, and it didn't occur to me that I was no longer a student. I was being paid by the army, so I could be financing my life on my own. But old (bad) habits die hard.

· · ·

In late January of 1944, Doc Horowitz and I were driving in his ambulance to Oxford, when we picked up a Wren (Women's Royal Naval Service) hitchhiker who was going back to her "Wrennery" at Faringdon, an old market town similar to Devizes. Petite and pretty, with a lovely smile and infectious laugh, she had an air of independence and wit, and I liked her immediately. A strong booster of the Wrens, she quickly taught Doc and me the popular ditty: "Say little Wren, when, when, when are you going to invite me to tea?" I decided then and there to see her as frequently as possible.

Being with Edna Glew in England made it come alive for me in ways that would never have occurred otherwise. "England is a thrilling place to be these days," I wrote home, and Edna was a major factor in making it so. She was a person of strong beliefs, voiced calmly but firmly, and I saw England through her eyes, which helped me understand what was taking place in the emotions and lives of her countrymen and women. The male members of her family, I learned, were long-term enlisted naval personnel, and I had the sense that she was a patriot born and bred. She was of the lowest rank in the Wrens, similar to a private in the army, but regardless of rank, she loved the service and was totally dedicated to it. And a low rank meant nothing to her—she was socially mobile, going with whoever and wherever she wished.

Our modus operandi was to trade off on visits, with her coming to Devizes one weekend, and me going to Faringdon the next, or, better yet, both of us meeting in London. Our first visit together, shortly after we met, was a dance in Devizes. At my request, Edna brought along a Wren friend from Faringdon named Joan Hills as a date for Tom Cooke, the Jersey boy. Joan was bright and lively with a wry, understated sense of humor and was comely to boot; it didn't take long for her to penetrate Tom's outward cynicism and for the two of them to fall deeply in love. So suited were they to each other,

I have never been able to understand why they didn't marry. But perhaps the same could be said of me and Edna.

Part of the attraction for the girls was more practical than romantic, it turns out. U.S. Army chow in England, lacking as it was in fresh staples compared to military fare in the States, was still far superior to British military kitchens in England. Although Tom Cooke and I were convinced that the lure of Devizes for our girlfriends was their hosts' great charm, Joan disabused me of this idea when we met many years after the war. "We loved coming to Devizes to see you and Tom," she said. "It was the only time we ever got fresh meat and vegetables."

The weekend after Joan and Tom first met, we journeyed to Faringdon to see our newfound friends, driven in a jeep by Corporal S., a quiet, mild-mannered soldier from the Deep South. On arriving, we booked two rooms at the doorstep of a cottage, one for Corporal S. and one for ourselves, and as we did so our landlady informed us that she had two other American soldiers staying there also, friends of her daughters. Thinking nothing of this, we had dinner with Edna and Joan and then S., Tom, and I returned to our cottage—and to an explosion. The "two other American soldiers" were black. The army in those days was still segregated, and S.'s mildness disappeared as he totally lost control in what he considered to be an unbearable situation. Refusing to remain under the same roof with these fellow soldiers, he stormed out to stay elsewhere. Cooke and I apologized to the two soldiers, who accepted the apologies gracefully, but the rancor that was generated stayed in the air. It was an unnecessarily unpleasant scene all around. I was not used to seeing young African American males socializing with young white females, but as

I watched them briefly in the house's living room it occurred to me that England had different mores, and that I had better get used to them. I felt that Corporal S.'s prejudiced tantrum was a wretched display, of which I disapproved on the deepest level of my being. I was coming to understand that hatred of the "other" on a mass level is what leads to tyranny; that blaming all of society's ills on the Jews is a large part of what catapulted Hitler to power.

. . .

One morning, at the start of February 1944, the division's approximately 500 officers were ordered to be on hand in full uniform at 8 a.m. in the Prince Maurice Barracks' Garrison Theater to meet our new army commander, whose name, for the moment, was unknown to us. When all of us were assembled and seated, someone shouted "Attention!" and we stood up and watched as down the theater's center aisle strode a pair of broad-shouldered, straight-backed six-footers: Major General "Tiger Jack" Wood, our division commander, followed by our new army commander, Lieutenant General George Patton.

General Wood approached the microphone and said: "Gentlemen, I am proud to introduce our army commander, the commanding general of the new Third United States Army, Lieutenant General George S. Patton, Jr.! General Patton is an old friend of mine since our days at West Point and, without doubt, the finest combat soldier in the army."

Then General Patton, wearing a glossy helmet with three stars on it and an immaculate beribboned uniform with two revolvers, stepped forward and said: "Be seated, gentlemen." The first surprise was his voice. Instead of the rich, authoritative baritone that I had expected, Patton's vocal tone was exceedingly high and squeaky. The theater audience sat motionless as he looked us over, and you could feel the tension. About six months earlier the papers had run exhaustive coverage of General Patton slapping a soldier in a hospital in Sicily and being relieved of the command of the Seventh U.S. Army as a result. Patton had become livid upon discovering that the enlisted man in the Sicilian hospital bed did not have an obvious wound, but instead had been hospitalized for "battle fatigue," a diagnosis the general found outrageous and entirely without merit. Though I could understand his point of view at the time—certainly the army had to be circumspect about the conditions under which they would allow soldiers to leave the battlefield—little did I know that in a few short months the condition that incited Patton's wrath would be grabbing me by the throat. Consistently, psychological trauma to soldiers is one of the big costs of going to war—a generation of survivors may have a great deal of difficulty returning to ordinary life, and there are significant medical and societal costs associated with this. But you rarely see it as a discussion point or budget line item when we debate the merits of a particular engagement. It's a grim reality that we'd rather deny or ignore.

Patton, tasked with facing the most formidable military machine the world had known, couldn't afford to lose even a single man unnecessarily. So he unleashed a slap that cost him a suspension. For five months now, he had been in limbo, and he was the most controversial soldier in the service.

His next words to us, officers who had never fought but knew about Patton's history, were not reassuring: "If you stand up on the battlefield like a wedding prick, you deserve to get shot," he said in his high shrill. And then, "I know a major who took hits from fifty-six machine-gun bullets be-cause he was stupid enough to stand up, and the son of a bitch is still alive." He continued on for a while longer, using extraordinary profanity. I have never heard such language be-fore or since as I did on the day when Patton addressed us. (I came home from the war using profanity myself, whether picked up from Patton or someone else, I don't know; to my dear wife's despair, I continue using it to this day.)

When we officers left the theater our feeling was one of be-musement: we didn't know whether Patton would affect our fortunes for good or bad. All we knew was that he was not your normal, run-of-the-mill type of person. But something was now sinking into our consciousness: the fact that our di-vision was no longer homeless but was, instead, part of a great new army, and that our new commander knew more about tanks than anyone else (with the possible exception of Erwin Rommel). Once combat began, our esteem for General Patton grew until it knew no bounds. In the next sixteen months I was destined to see Patton three more times and to talk to him (in short conversations, to be sure) on two of those occasions.

. . .

A few months after meeting General Patton, I found myself in London. It was June 6, 1944, and Edna and I were at the theater, enjoying a matinee performance of Cole Porter's *Panama Hattie,* which starred a married pair of American ac-tors, Bebe Daniels and Ben Lyon, when suddenly the curtain dropped. A somber stage manager rolled a radio onto the pro-scenium, and the audience sat in stunned silence listening to an address by King George VI announcing that the invasion of France by the Allies had begun.

D-Day was a monumental operation. Code-named Operation Neptune, it remains to this day the largest seaborne invasion in history. On the first day alone, we lost some 10,000 men. Though our attack was focused on the beaches of Normandy, the Allied command had devoted considerable resources to a smoke-screen plan to convince the Nazis that we'd be striking from Dover to Calais, the narrowest point of the English Channel. To bolster this ploy, we had created a fictional "First United States Army Group," complete with inflatable tanks and fake machinery. Its leader was none other than George Patton, whose skills were well known to the Germans.

These were facts I'd learn long after the war. All I knew, as I sat in rapt attention that afternoon with Edna in the West End theater, was that the situation had suddenly gotten very real. We glanced at one another silently, and without saying a word, we both knew: everything was about to change.

As King George VI continued his speech, he declared: "On this momentous occasion, we in Britain are honored and grateful to have the courageous troops from the U.S. as our allies." A catcall came from the back of the theater: "You damn well ought to be, you limey SOB!"

I was appalled. I simply could not believe what I was hearing. I knew it was just more of that macho swagger to masquerade the disquieting fear that was now growing inside all of us and over which we had no control. But what an inopportune time to insult our hosts! The Brits had been hanging tough against the Nazi juggernaut for years before we became involved. Shuddering inwardly, I experienced a sense of deep discomfort about my fellow Americans—and myself.

I returned to Devizes from London to be handed a letter from General Eisenhower addressed to the "Soldiers, Sailors and Airmen of the Allied Expeditionary Force." It read as follows:

> You are about to embark upon the Great Crusade. . . . The eyes of the world are upon you. The hopes and prayers of liberty-loving people everywhere march with you. In company with our brave Allies . . . you will bring about the destruction of the German war machine, the elimination of Nazi tyranny over the oppressed peoples of Europe, and security for ourselves in a free world.
>
> Your task will not be an easy one. Your enemy is well trained, well equipped and battle-hardened. He will fight savagely. . . .
>
> I have full confidence in your courage, devotion to duty and skill in battle. We will accept nothing less than full Victory.
>
> Good Luck! And let us all beseech the blessing of Almighty God upon this great and noble undertaking.

Two weeks prior, members of the division had received a short letter from Major General John S. Wood, along similar lines:

> We have met every test of war itself except enemy fire, and we have prepared ourselves for that. . . .
>
> We have hardened and toughened ourselves for battle. We can march, maneuver, and shoot to kill. . . . The hour is at hand!

But, in fact, it would be another four weeks before the 10,000 men of our Fourth Armored Division would join the initial invasion force in France. It was odd (and frustrating) to be still living comfortably in the Prince Maurice Barracks while our fellow soldiers were battling on the beaches in Normandy. In our naiveté, we were eager to join the fight, not fully fathoming that men were dying by the thousands.

Despite the high-stakes drama across the Channel, it was still the same old situation for the 94th, dances and all. I wrote several letters to my parents describing this strange normalcy in mid-June:

> We're having a dance tonight, probably our last . . . here we are, having a great time, while boys from the divisions that used to be around us are fighting for their lives in Normandy. Some cockeyed world!

> Am typing from our command post tent, which is my office. Sitting around reading are Col. Graham, Maj. Parker, and Capt. Cooke. The Colonel is laughing at the cartoon called "Sad Sack" in Yank magazine . . . really very funny.

In retrospect, there's something funny about my correspondence with my family during this period. In all of my letters home from England, I never described Edna or referred to her by name. I was undoubtedly fearful of my mother's and grandmother's overly critical views: *What's her background? Is she well educated? Could she move in our circles? Is she anti-Semitic? Is her family well-off?* etc. When it came to bucking what I thought Larie's and Annie's opinions might be, I was gutless and played it safe: no names, ladies—to you, she's a cipher.

However, on June 30, in my last letter from Devizes, I made an effort to describe Edna:

> The last week has been one of the nicest for me. . . . The Wren spent her leave here and I saw her every night. Strictly a swell, clean gal . . . and darn nice company . . . she's one of

the best I've ever met, a real straight shooter, good sense of humor, et al. Tom and I were lucky.

I certainly got the last sentence right: Tom and I were extremely lucky. Edna and Joan were just about two of the loveliest and most intelligent women we could possibly have met.

Joan, Tom, Edna, and I had always known that the four of us would have to part unexpectedly, without much prior notice. But we didn't anticipate that it would be as abrupt as it turned out to be. Suddenly, we received super-secret orders to move to the Channel, and I remember telephoning Edna for a cryptic conversation: "You and Joan, please do not come down here this weekend."

She replied, "Oh, I see. Of course." As I heard her two British stiff-upper-lip sentences, I realized that our period of English enchantment had ended.

The Fourth Armored did what was called a move-out from the Prince Maurice Barracks and traveled about seventy miles south to the small Channel-coast town of Weymouth, making camp in pup tents and then doing nothing. We could no longer use telephones. Although we could write letters, we were ordered to say nothing about what was taking place. Here's what I wrote to my dad:

> All of our thoughts are on the future. We'll be in battle one of these days—for the first time. I know I'm going to be very scared, but I hope that I can do a good job and be of some use to the rest of the guys and a help to the men. Of course, we all of us feel that we'll come through O.K.—but there is an element of risk. Anyway, I want you to know how much I love you & Mom & Gogs [my grandmother] & how

swell you've all been. God willing, someday we'll be together again.

Loaded to the gills with equipment, we crossed the Channel at night on July 10, 1944. Spirits soaring. And scared as hell.

Bty. Area - Base Camp

Camp Ibis, a training center in the Mojave Desert, in 1943. En route to this camp I inadvertently went AWOL, causing me to be "grounded" for a month.

In front of my tent in the Mojave Desert in early 1943. My time in the Mojave was exciting and productive—the opposite of Fort Bragg. I was a happy camper in the Mojave.

With Lieutenants Charlie Gillens and Darrell Wood in the Mojave Desert. Charlie and I became lasting friends.

Lieutenant Don Guild in the Mojave Desert. Guild, a forward observer, was outstanding in combat.

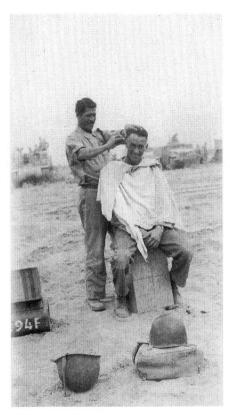

The improvised
barbershop in the
Mojave Desert.

My gun battery ("C" Battery) in the Mojave Desert. The battalion had three gun
batteries, each with six 105mm howitzers.

.50 cal M.G.

105 mm. how

A closer look at our self-propelled half-tracks with their 105mm howitzers and .50 caliber machine guns.

In front of a self-propelled 105mm howitzer in the Mojave Desert. In contrast to the infantry, where the guns were towed on a platform, our howitzers were motorized, making them highly mobile.

With my buddies (from left): Lieutenants Charlie Gillens, me, Bill Lothian, and John Kelly in the Mojave Desert, 1943. Gillens and Lothian were gun battery officers, while Kelly and I were forward observers. We all got along extremely well.

Captain Bob Parker, the commander of my "C" Battery in the Mojave Desert. Early on, Parker and I became close friends, a friendship that lasted a lifetime.

Lieutenant Colonel Alex Graham, my battalion commander, in the Mojave Desert. I loved Graham, a delightful person and a model West Point soldier if there ever was one.

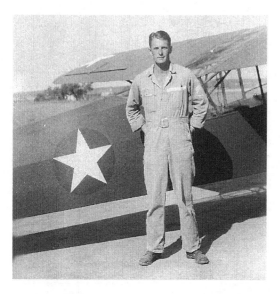

Sergeant Harley Merrick at his flying school in Texas. An outstanding forward observer pilot, he rose to the rank of major. We became lifelong friends.

With Billie Brandt, my first real girlfriend, at El Rancho hotel in Las Vegas, 1943. We only dated for a few months before my battalion was sent off to Camp Bowie in Texas.

After I finally made it overseas to British shores, I met Wren Edna Frances Glew in early 1944. She made England come alive for me during the many months I was stationed there. (Unfortunately my camera was stolen in England, so I have no more photos until after the war.)

# 9

# I BEGIN KILLING THE ENEMY

**AS WE CROSSED THE ENGLISH CHANNEL** in our LST (Landing Ship, Tank), the air was full of brine. And there was another smell that I couldn't quite put my finger on: an acrid odor. It hung above us—500 men, laden with gear and crammed tight on the deck of the amphibious landing craft, with tension thick enough to slice. Suddenly it occurred to me that this olfactory sensation permeating the air was perhaps a window into our animal nature. I was smelling the fear!

Not that we'd encounter the types of defensive positions that our brothers had braved when they stormed the Normandy beaches one month earlier—where German turrets on the palisades mowed down GIs by the hundreds. Many of the men died on the boats, others while wading ashore. We had all read the accounts of Operation Neptune—and I was mighty relieved that we wouldn't be facing *that* kind of mayhem. Nonetheless, once we got off the boats and stepped onto that beach, we'd be in hostile territory, which meant that at any given moment, a bullet could find its way into my anatomy.

The Normandy beaches were roughly 200 miles northwest of Paris, which was now under German occupation along with the rest of France. The Hotel Majestic had been seized by the Nazis to serve as the headquarters of the Wehrmacht high command; that's where I had stayed as a thirteen-year-old tourist and where George Gershwin, in 1928, had composed "An American in Paris." But the City of Light had dimmed considerably since the German army goose-stepped its way down the Champs Élysées. It was now a place of furtive glances and anxious whispers, under the watchful eyes of the Gestapo. If we wanted to get an American back into Paris, we'd have to fight our way in.

I was feeling confident about our prospects of doing so, a confidence based in great part on the faith I had in my fellow officers and in General John S. Wood, our division commander, who was universally worshipped by his troops. We had good leadership, we had had eighteen months of solid training, and we had the moral high ground. No one was suggesting it would be easy, but certainly we had every reason to believe we would prevail.

Our confidence vanished, however, and our spirits plummeted when we landed on Utah Beach. Moving ashore from our LST, I was aghast at what hit my eyes on the dunes—a long line of stretchers as far as the eye could see, with wounded soldiers on every one of them, moaning in pain or crying as they waited for relief. This was the Allied beachhead, the point of resupply and evacuation. It's where every badly injured soldier (thousands of them daily) would be taken to be loaded onto boats for medical attention in British hospitals. I stared speechlessly at the panorama before me, having trouble digesting it—the sheer numbers of badly injured young men, soldiers just like me, now missing limbs. And this didn't even reflect the KIA, the killed in action, or the thousands more who had been triaged on the battlefield—allowed to expire after a brief instant of relief with a morphine syrette. The cost of war had been suddenly laid out in grotesque clarity. For us new arrivals, this scene on the beach was a vivid and terrifying illustration of what we now faced. The unexpected pang of fear was sudden and intense. I had to remind myself that this was a friendly beach—one that we controlled. No enemy fire, no real danger. Ahead of me lay a long series of actual battlefields, and they could not be ducked. The only possible way out was to have Doc [Earl] Mericle, the division psychiatrist, certify you as unfit for battle, and though I was full of fear, seeing Doc Mericle was one step I did not contemplate.

In the most severe cases, Mericle had the discretion to relieve a soldier of duty and send him home in what was known as a "Section Eight" discharge. This actually happened to some of us. Our original survey officer, Lieutenant W., a competent and personable soldier whom I had always liked for his straightforwardness and soldierly demeanor, crumbled in combat and quietly disappeared from our midst. Whether or not he actually was unable to function, only Doc Mericle could determine. But, in our minds, when we noticed W.'s absence and found out what had happened, he was forever disgraced. And yet he may well have lived a long and happy life. As I gazed numbly at the endless line of stretchers on the windswept dunes, I worried suddenly about my own prospects for longevity.

Fortunately, we didn't linger on that beach. The battalion soon marched to higher ground as we prepared to make camp in a field not far from the village of Barneville. Then something happened that was unexpected and, frankly, bizarre. We found ourselves surrounded by the local citizenry, who were thrilled to greet the American liberators and who thrust bottles of calvados (we were in apple orchard country) upon us. After the disquieting moment on the beach, most of us were more than happy to partake in the local apple brandy. Within a short time, our battalion was dead drunk.

To be going into combat with 500 men unable to function was no joke, and here was a perfect example of Alex Graham's grace under pressure. Without the slightest hint of panic, our teetotaling colonel acted fast to bring about sobriety. He divided the battalion, sober or otherwise, into a number of circles, and then ordered the circles to start running. When we were exhausted, he called a halt and black coffee was served. Somehow or other, almost everyone was able to function from then on.

As of July 11, 1944—the day we landed—the Third Army had not been activated so we were attached as support artillery to the Fourth Infantry Division, which had been fighting steadily since D-Day. That was just a month or so earlier, but it may as well have been ten years. To our innocent eyes, the battle-hardened soldiers of the Fourth looked liked they had been to hell and back. Their weary faces were smeared with mud and memories that would haunt them for a lifetime. These men were legends; their ranks included the likes of Ernest Hemingway (with the 22nd Infantry Regiment) and J. D. Salinger (with the 12th). They were the first to land on Utah Beach and charge headlong into the blizzard of bullets from the German fortified bunkers, the first to hopscotch in terror across the booby-trapped beach and then storm the fortified cliffs. Eventually, they'd pierce the left flank of the German Seventh Army and march on to liberate Paris. But for now, they were locked in a deadly stalemate in the Normandy "hedgerow country," a place noted for the intense difficulty of moving through its hedges—whether brush, brambles, or dense fruit orchards, it was totally impassible for army vehicles.

In fact, when the Fourth Armored Division arrived with our tanks and half-tracks, we were completely stymied. Our vehicles could not advance even an inch as long as the Germans controlled the roads with their mortars and dug-in artillery; hence, our battalions were assigned to provide relief for the exhausted Fourth Infantry Division. They desperately needed to be rotated out for some well-deserved R&R, while we took over their positions. That meant that the two Bills—Lothian and Walsh—plus Click, our third battery commander, along with their men, would be replacing some of the Fourth Infantry's gun batteries, and they'd need forward observers like me to sneak into the treacherous hedgerows, careful to avoid mines and sniper fire, but getting close enough to spot the enemy and instruct the batteries where to shoot. The forward observers in the 94th included myself, John Kelly, Lewis "Dude" Dent, a famous college football star, and eight others. No one was too eager to be the first FO assigned to go to the front. We had all seen those wounded bodies on the beach; we knew the stakes.

Though only a year older than me, Dude Dent had married the campus beauty queen at Colorado A&M and already had two children; John Kelly, my pal from New York and slightly older than the rest of us, was likewise hitched. Despite their ties back home, I, sadly, would be the only one of this trio to survive the war. But it wouldn't end just yet for Dent and Kelly—they were not the ones chosen this morning to venture into the murderous hedgerows.

On this—our first day in battle—Harvard youngster Bob Parker, now a major and the third ranker in our battalion (whose job it was to dole out assignments), chose an unlucky lieutenant named George Powell. Parker explained to us that all FO assignments would be on a rotating basis—when it's your turn, you go, no questions, no complaints. Lieutenant Powell, the first man in the rotation, had no choice. So off he went with his support team, scrambling stealthily toward the German position.

It struck me as a curious thing, how in war we can override our primal instincts to do what we have to do. Instead of running away from danger, we push forward, scared but not reluctant. Here was Second Lieutenant Powell, a freshman at combat, creeping toward the Germans, with just a hedgerow in between, bullets whizzing overhead and explosions everywhere. He kept going, but it did not end well for him.

Somehow Powell was spotted and captured within a matter of hours. Next in the rotation was First Lieutenant Bertil Nystrom, someone we all admired, but he, too, was unlucky. An incoming mortar exploded near where he was positioned, wounding him badly. So Nystrom was evacuated on a stretcher back to Utah Beach (along with the countless other soldiers who fell that day), to be taken for treatment in England.

I'm not sure who went after him, but I'm certainly glad it wasn't me. I had been ordered that morning to go on a different mission—reconnoitering the hedgerow country around our flank to ensure that there were no stray Germans in the area. Each of us FOs had been assigned a driver, a radioman, and a sergeant to be part of our unit. I took my sergeant, Bob Plas, on that reconnaissance with me.

Carbine and rifle at the ready, we ventured into the hedgerows. In the quiet between bursts of distant gunfire, I could hear crickets and other sounds of nature. Indeed, as we moved farther away from our unit, the noises of war receded in the distance and I found myself experiencing an emotion I hadn't expected: joy.

This countryside was beautiful beyond belief—plentiful fruit orchards connected by narrow, winding dirt roads with lovely trees on either side. It was a coastal paradise, albeit a rugged one, so enticing that I almost forgot that the enemy was right there; any second we could walk into a sniper's sightline or encounter some Germans separated from their units. For a few brief moments, this wondrous sight of nature got the better of me. I couldn't resist the low-hanging fresh fruit, within tantalizing arm's reach. I would dart over to a tree, grab a few pieces, and run, hoping not to be spotted.

As Sergeant Plas and I continued through this orchard bliss, we rounded a corner of our tree-lined road. We heard German voices nearby—suddenly, we spotted two Wehrmacht soldiers walking toward us! They were conversing nonchalantly with one another, unaware of our presence. The sergeant and I raised our guns and shouted, ordering them to halt. But they didn't. Just kept walking in our direction. It happened so fast. We pulled our triggers. They fell.

For a moment, I couldn't quite believe what had just transpired. I was one of the best shots in the battalion, so I was pretty sure my man was dead. The other enemy soldier appeared to be equally motionless. Sergeant Plas and I exchanged an unspoken glance. Suddenly and unexpectedly, we had begun killing the enemy. I was never quite the same afterward.

A thousand questions raced through my mind. Had they not heard us? Were the sergeant and I threatened? Was it necessary to do what we did? Could we have disarmed and captured them? God only knows.

I'm not sure how else we could have handled the situation. Maybe a more experienced soldier would have come up with a better solution. It was my first day in battle, my very first encounter with German soldiers; I had been given that carbine only two weeks before. Moments earlier, in all likelihood, those two Germans were getting swept up by the orchard paradise just like I had been, which would explain why they didn't notice us. And because we spotted them before they saw us, they were now face down in the dirt—while we were on our feet. My head was spinning.

Here I was finally in Europe—after obstacles, reassignments, delays—finally fighting the Nazi forces, finally doing my part to defeat Hitler, and what am I feeling about it? Guilty! It's the last thing I expected.

Within a short time, the act of killing became almost routine to us, which made me feel even guiltier. But it was a matter of survival: kill or be killed. Simple as that. The situation with those two Germans in the hedgerows could have easily been reversed. They could have spotted us first, and this memoir would never have come to be. But would they have felt guilty about it like I did?

The outrageousness of war struck me hard, even if I didn't fully process it at the time, and has remained with me ever since. The casualness and ease of pulling a trigger and ending an enemy soldier's life could made you believe that what you had done was of little consequence, especially when it's not up-close and personal. That's why technological developments in armaments have been about increasing the space between you and the enemy soldier you're expected to kill, so the act of killing becomes more removed.

In hand-to-hand combat, he was right there: eye to eye. A sword allowed you to take a step back, a spear you could throw from a distance, a bow and arrow gave you even greater range. Then came gunpowder, pistols, rifles, and cannons. With long-range artillery, you can be miles away from the people you kill and never even see them. With missiles and drones, you can be halfway across the world. It makes it a lot easier to push that button, which is why hawks love this stuff. War is about killing. The greater the enemy casualties, the better it is for your side. But soldiers on the ground—even the victors— always pay a price.

Now that we were in the thick of it, we referred to the Germans as "krauts" and wholeheartedly believed that a good German was a dead German. For me, an American soldier of Jewish background, this was especially true. They would have unquestionably killed me if they had won. I felt adamant that the Nazis had to be stopped at all costs. This pathological hatred of all things German was, it now seems to me, irrational, but back then it was literally my religion, and I became more and more tolerant of violence—my own violent acts and the violence inflicted on others. My mind-set was: it has to be done. And so it was, night and day. Kill or be killed.

It made us all skittish, fingers constantly on our triggers. One afternoon in Coutances, a careening ammunition cart hitched to a runaway German horse came racing down a village road and took us by surprise. It was me, Alex Graham, and Sergeant Plas. My sergeant, unaware that there were no Germans on the cart, opened fire and hit the horse. As it lay dying, Graham, grief-stricken, went almost berserk. After berating Sergeant Plas in a manner so severe and enraged that I am sure Plas was never able to forget it, Graham shot the horse and left us. And never, by word or manner, did he refer to the incident again. The only time I ever witnessed Graham lose his cool, it illustrated how no one is fully inured to the pressures of combat.

. . .

Being shot at by the Germans was the name of the game from July 1944 through May 1945, a time of almost continuous combat. Receiving fire was absolutely terrifying, and although we got used to it as an inevitability, we were never, ever free from the fear of it. Sometimes it came from above. While we were immobilized, stuck like sitting ducks, in the Normandy hedgerows, the German air force strafed us with rockets, machine guns, and, occasionally, bombs. But even that was manageable somehow—because we could see and hear where they were coming from, and we would see them recede as they flew by overhead. Not so with an artillery bombardment. It was unclear where it was coming from or where it would land—a long climax and a sudden sickening crunch. An artillery round was not something you could duck like a bullet; those shells left craters. It was Russian roulette every time you heard that horrendous sound, and mortars were even worse. Those shells soared up into the sky in a sweeping arc with a creepy sound that felt like it was coming from everywhere. The whistle had an eerie aspect to it, increasing in intensity as it approached—without a doubt the most awful noise I've ever heard. But there were degrees of mortar awfulness. By far the worst were the *Nebelwerfers,* or "screaming meemies," as we called them. They turned my blood cold. Volleys came in at five-second intervals, and there was nothing you could do but pray. If you happened to be at the receiving end of that projectile's parabola, you were toast.

And it wasn't only the Germans who hurt us—we sometimes hurt ourselves. Before the Third Army broke out of Normandy, the U.S. Air Force accidentally bombed and killed Lieutenant General Lesley J. McNair, a top U.S. Army commander. My battalion may also have been responsible for a "friendly fire" incident—and that's when my guilt went into overdrive.

. . .

I remember clear as a bell the first time I looked into the eyes of a Nazi. We'd been locked in the hedgerows for several days, going nowhere. This static situation was an aberration. Ten days from now, we'd punch through the German defense line at Avranches and hardly stop for the next eleven months. As the Third Army's leading unit, the Fourth Armored Division was almost always on the go. Patton moved faster than most, if not all, other army commanders, and our mantra, repeated endlessly, was: "Keep moving!"

Not so, in Normandy. The Germans didn't budge, and their intractable position kept us from moving forward. While our battalion was stuck in this stalemate, firing intermittently, my team and I captured some German soldiers, one of whom was a junior-grade officer. I had not seen Germans up-close since my boyhood, and never ones wearing Wehrmacht uniforms. From what I'd read about the regime, I regarded the Nazis as subhuman. I had the chance now to make that assessment with my own eyes, so I took my time, getting a good long look at the "kraut" POWs.

The German enlisted men seemed much like ours—tired, somewhat beaten up, but otherwise normal human beings. The junior lieutenant, however, was sullen, angry, and glared at me almost arrogantly with his steely blue eyes. Typical Nazi bastard, I thought.

Then I wondered: what's he thinking about me? Yankee SOB. Or worse? Could he sense that I was Jewish? No, not possible. But Jewish or not, there's no question he felt utter disdain toward me and my comrades. As he should have, I suppose. War doesn't work unless we dehumanize our enemy through propaganda, so that we can take their lives without guilt. Kraut, Jap, Gook, Commie. Not like us. Not human.

. . .

Shortly after these prisoners were captured, some enlisted men and I went into a nearby forest of tall firs looking for more Germans. Curiously, we heard neighing and bells ringing, and soon came across a ravine in which a long line of pack animals, both horses and mules, were standing unattended. Each animal had a pair of wooden boxes strapped to its back. When we opened one of the boxes (I would guess there were over one hundred of them in this pack train), we found it full of money! The cases were filled to the brim with stacks of French francs. It was like a scene from a movie. We had probably stumbled on a division's pay train—confiscated French currency, with which the German army was paying its troops.

We quickly got hold of a jeep and loaded it down with boxes to bring back to the battalion. Then, at my suggestion, we passed the francs out to anyone who wanted some until they were distributed throughout the battalion. I felt, for a moment, like Santa Claus. Later we received an opinion from the division finance officer that the francs were worthless, so we called them "funny money," and, from Avranches on, we threw them out of our half-track vehicles at all and sundry French passersby as we moved along. But the finance officer was dead wrong; the francs were solidly supported, and about a month later the ones still left were redeemed at full value. We pack-train discoverers had casually tossed away a fortune.

It was great to finally be moving, however. After fighting our way through Coutances, Periers, and La Haye-Pesnel, on July 31, 1944, our armored vehicles rolled into Avranches, a town of 7,000 set on high ground overlooking the coastal marshes.

The picturesque village dating back to Roman times was a pale shadow of its former self. From my jeep I saw devastation all around me, smoke pouring from the battered ruins. We came upon an MP (military police) directing traffic, and he signaled us to turn to the right. As we made the turn we came upon the Avranches town square, where a parked command car was facing us.

On the hood stood the most inspiring sight I have ever seen: a man in an immaculate uniform wearing black boots, a shiny helmet, and a pistol on either hip. He stood straight as an arrow, smiled, and saluted each of us before we could salute him. It was, of course, General Patton, standing amid all this devastation and terror. He looked positively buoyant as he cheered us on.

There are things I have learned since about Patton, among them that he was an anti-Semite. But I have never changed my mind about him. At a time in my life when reassurance was at a premium, there it was in the person of my army commander, and there he was saluting—me!

Patton became the personification of the United States Army at its best, a leader at the front sharing our risk and showing us the way forward. Seeing him standing there amid the smoking ruins was inspirational and made me and the others wholeheartedly ready to follow him anywhere.

# 10

# "ABANDON POST!"

**NONE OF US KNEW THE BIG PICTURE.** Strategic objectives were left to the generals. All we knew was where we were going next, and sometimes not even that. It was a chain-of-command thing: the higher up you went the more you were told.

To be always on the move with things changing daily was somewhat disorienting. We hardly stayed in one place long enough to get a true feel for it. Demographics and geography became a blur. Whether a place we passed was a village, a town, or a city usually could not be ascertained. We went from Avranches to Rennes to Vannes to Caudan and stopped short of Lorient, and if you had asked me which were big and which small I could not have told you. At the time, we all thought Vannes (25,000) and Rennes (110,000) were about the same size. In Belgium we went from Arlon to Bastogne, and I would have guessed respective populations of 3,000 and 50,000. In fact, Arlon was 17,000 and Bastogne 5,000.

When we were still stationary in Normandy, before breaking out at Avranches, we had been joined by a group of French paramilitary known as the French Forces of the Interior (FFI). I think many of them had been in the French underground before D-Day; now they were being attached to various combat units to provide local intelligence. They certainly wanted to help and were definitely on our side, but in time we came to regard them as troublesome, a pain in the neck. They asked all sorts of questions and gave constant advice about everything. Their English was terrible and our French even worse, so that communication between them and us was garbled and difficult. The head FFIer in the group assigned to our battalion reported to me in my role as adjutant. "I speaks seven languages," he used to say, "and English I spokes the best."

Alex Graham recognized the language barrier as a problem, and his move to solve it was to appoint me as the battalion translator. I did know more French than the rest of the battalion, excluding Graham—a teacher of French at West Point—but that wasn't saying much. I had had a tutor, Mlle. Nadine Burton, when I was nine or ten, and received a weekly lesson at home. But we concentrated on grammar rather than conversation or vocabulary, and I didn't learn or retain much. I had picked up a little bit more when I had visited France as a boy in 1935, but the net result was a rather pitiful performance. Nonetheless, I was now the official battalion linguist, sought out by one and all whenever a language problem came up in France.

Conversation with French citizens and later with those of Belgium and Luxembourg was, of necessity, brief; we seldom stopped moving. So my "talents" as battalion translator were infrequently called upon. "How do you say, 'Will you trade a fresh egg for a bar of chocolate?'" was a typical question. But every so often I was asked a question about the location of the enemy or how to find a certain crossroad or bridge shown on our maps but which, for some reason, we could not find on the ground (as our maps were quite frequently in error). Because map reading had become one of my better army skills, I was often used to ask the locals for a missing landmark.

Our relationship with the French often placed us as the recipients of their adulation for having rid them of their much-feared oppressors. And usually this adulation was accompanied by gifts of flowers, wine, cognac, fruit, and baked goods. But there was also the reverse: continual roadside requests from French youngsters and adults alike for cigarettes and chocolate, which were impossible to obtain in France at that time. In certain small towns we would get looks from one and all of skepticism, looks that said, "Who are you guys?" And every so often I would come across a family who regarded me with suspicion, if not outright hostility. I remember, for example, going into a house in the Brittany countryside where there were four or five people, attractive, alert, and definitely a cut above middle class. Their faces said: "We don't like you. Leave us." What the problem was I never knew, but it made a long-lasting impression on me.

A day or so before we were to attack Rennes, the leader of our FFI unit told me that the Germans had abandoned it and that there would be no opposition—information that I passed on to my superiors. Expecting smooth sailing, the 35th Tank Battalion, 10th Infantry Battalion, and 66th Artillery Battalion were taken by surprise when they suddenly came under intense fire from eight emplaced-in-concrete 88mm guns—the finest weapon the Germans possessed. Not only was our FFI unit dead wrong about the Germans having evacuated their position at Rennes, it turned out the Wehrmacht had a gunnery school there, which meant that the formidable 88mm guns were dug in, perched up high in ideal firing positions to pick us off as we rolled across the exposed plain.

To come under fire like that was absolutely terrifying. Though we had heard rumors about the storied weapons, this was the first time we'd actually faced them up-close. These guns had originally been designed for use as anti-aircraft batteries, so their projectiles were highly efficient and exploded from the muzzles at breakneck velocities. But they were a dual-purpose weapon. Not only could they be aimed up in the air, they had a "down" level, where they aimed at our tanks, seeming to penetrate the heavy armor as if it were butter. Indeed, the 88s became known as "tank killers." By contrast, our 105mm howitzers were far less effective against the German panzers.

The German defense of Rennes was impressive, particularly since they were outnumbered and we controlled the air. They inflicted real damage with their 88s before going down to defeat. But I wasn't there to see it. My division was ordered to get to Lorient on the coast, so we broke off and moved around Rennes to head south. An infantry division replaced us, and a day or so later captured the city. Still, after Rennes, no one in the Fourth Armored could ever shake off dread of the 88s. And we got rid of those FFI advisers like hot potatoes.

. . .

Attacking Rennes had been like stepping into a nest of rattlesnakes; imagine our surprise and delight, then, when we arrived in Vannes to find it unoccupied and completely at our disposal. My memory is of a beautiful place with a citizenry that was thrilled to see us and wonderfully hospitable. Our timing was perfect. The division had to stop and prepare a strategy of just where and how to attack Lorient, and while this was going on we had two days of R&R in Vannes: swimming, showering, sleeping, even picnicking—all under the kindly, loving eyes of our hosts, the Vannes townspeople.

I wrote home on September 2, 1944, in glowing terms:

Had a helluva time taking Rennes but the Boche capitulated without a fight in Vannes. Tom Cooke, Lothian, and I rode into the city in a jeep preceding the battalion. We were about the first Americans they'd seen in five years and the French went nuts. . . . Gals hanging all over the jeep—people shoving wine at us, etc. Oh boy!

. . .

Those gals on our jeeps soon became distant memories when the shooting began again the following day, and I very nearly lost my life. The objective of this battle was to capture Lorient, a strategic seaport where the Germans had their U-boats in pens. But before committing troops to the battlefield, the U.S. command tried another tactic. Ordered, I believe, by General Patton—I don't think he would have had the hubris to do it on his own—General Wood sent a radio message to the German commander at Lorient demanding his surrender. When no affirmative response was received, we attacked their emplacements outside of the city.

My artillery battalion went into position not far from Lorient, near a very small town called Caudan (population 2,000). Our job was to support Colonel Creighton Abrams's blistering 37th Tank Battalion, which was leading the attack. The job of the artillery was to set up our eighteen howitzers in range of the enemy's guns or enemy troop movement. We'd need a forward observer to spot these positions, of course—and as luck would have it, it was my turn.

Major Parker ordered me and my support team to find the highest available perch for an observation post (OP). I surveyed the area and spotted something in the distance—a church steeple at the center of the nearby town. Perfect.

Or at least I thought it was perfect. You got up there with a pair of field binoculars and could see the entire panorama. The Germans had to survey a huge landscape, so even though it was probably the highest structure, they wouldn't necessarily know we were there. Sure, there was the risk that, with only one way in and out of a bell tower, a rapid evacuation might not be easy. And there was always the danger that my binoculars or another piece of glass could catch the sun and give us away. But every place has its risks. I was totally preoccupied that morning with wanting to do a good job in my debut as forward observer in an actual battle (putting aside the disheartening realization that I had somehow fallen into one of the most dangerous jobs in the army).

Once we went into action any fears seemed to disappear. Excited to be taking up our first observation post, my team drove furtively to Caudan's main square in our jeep. After parking quietly in an alley, the three of us—Sergeant Plas with his radio, my corporal with his telephone, and me with my map and binoculars—climbed the dusty, winding steps of the timeworn tower to emerge at the thirty-foot top of the church steeple.

The view was breathtaking. And I could easily make out the Germans' artillery positions from their gun flashes. Keyed up, I got to work, plotting out coordinates and barking them out to Plas, who radioed the firing orders back to our three batteries of six guns each.

Of course, as soon as we began shooting, my German counterpart (wherever he was hiding) would observe the flashes of *our* guns and would start telling his gun batteries where to shoot back. Pretty soon the entire valley was filled with the booming thunder of artillery. And that's how it was all morning. Fire. Counterfire. Fire. Counterfire.

The OPs all had one constant: the focus was on the enemy, and not the slightest attention was paid to the civilians in the area or their habitat. We'd often find that the enemy artillery and mortars were next to farmhouses or village homes or in streets or town structures in which civilian noncombatants might be living or working. Yet during the war, I cannot recall anyone ever giving any thought to protecting enemy civilians; our role was to rout the enemy military. If enemy civilians (collateral damage, in today's jargon) lost their lives—so be it. We never stopped adhering to our mantra: a good German is a dead German.

By mid-afternoon, my shots were improving. I had a pretty good fix on where to aim, but just as I was feeling confident that we could soon take out some of their batteries, it got dark. Major Parker ordered us to stop firing. After nightfall, firing your artillery makes you an easy target—as the muzzle flashes can be seen easily for miles. Thus, we had a de facto cease-fire till dawn.

My team and I snuck back to the jeep and returned to our unit to bed down for the night. I threw down my bedroll in the corner of a barn and shut my eyes, both exhausted and exhilarated. Even though the artillery bombardment had ceased, there continued to be small arms fire—the occasional rat-a-tat-tat of a machine-gun burst or a solitary sniper shell ricocheting off a wall. But my mind, amazingly, was able to tune all of that out—to label it "distant danger," not imminent—allowing me to slumber in peace. We had been at this for three weeks, and, while certainly not grizzled like the Fourth Infantry, we were now *actual* combat veterans.

. . .

The following morning Sergeant Plas shook me awake with a cup of coffee. It was an hour before dawn—time to get going. I reported to Lieutenant Colonel Graham, who asked me where I planned to set up today's OP. I told him I intended to return to the bell tower, which, in my view, had been an ideal position from which to observe the action. The thought seemed to intrigue him, and Graham announced suddenly that he was going to join us.

While artillery commanders tend to stay behind the front lines so they can supervise the guns, I could certainly see why Graham might have wanted to get an overview of the battlefield—to see the actual impact of our shelling and the counterfire from the enemy guns. Though he was more than ten years my senior and far higher in rank, it occurred to me that this was Lieutenant Colonel Graham's first time in front-line combat, just like me. He wanted to observe the battlefield to glean information that could improve both his understanding and skills as an artillery commander.

So off we went—six of us, including the two drivers—moving through the pre-light of dawn to the town square in Caudan. Darting quietly up three stories to the top of the bell tower, I unfurled my map and got to work. Feeling proud to have the colonel at my side, I pointed out the landmarks that I had spotted the day before—the places I had calculated as likely enemy artillery positions. Graham nodded and, after checking them out with his own binoculars, ordered me to begin the bombardment.

The shooting began and, once again, the plain erupted in artillery explosions. Trying to stay calm under the added pressure of having the CO breathing down my neck, I adjusted my firing coordinates and within short order felt pretty certain to have taken out at least one enemy battery. But that's when, suddenly, the tables turned. They started firing at us! German shells began coming in from an artillery battery I hadn't spotted earlier, one with a closer vantage point—which meant I could easily see its muzzle flashes.

Since their rounds were missing us, I decided to return fire, quickly calculating coordinates and having Plas radio them back. My first shot missed. They fired back at us. It was harrowing having shells fly in our direction, whizzing by the steeple.

I quickly shouted out an angle correction, which Plas radioed back to our battalion. These firing exchanges were hair-raising. Who would blink first? Then one of their shells grazed the outside of the steeple, causing bits of masonry to fall, crashing thirty feet to the ground.

"Abandon post!" I shouted suddenly, allowing Sergeant Plas and my corporal to descend the narrow stairwell before me. I gestured to Lieutenant Colonel Graham to do likewise, and we hightailed it as fast as we could down the winding steps, spurting to safety in the nick of time. The German artillery struck a direct hit on the upper part of the steeple, which came crashing down into a pile of rubble.

My eyes widened as I tried to catch my breath, adrenaline coursing through my veins. That was close. My mind began deconstructing the sequence of events, wondering how they had spotted us in the first place, since we certainly were not firing any weapons from the tower. Then it occurred to me: the Germans must have picked up a flashing reflection of the sun off my binoculars. It had been a close call, but the fact that it took the enemy over twenty-four hours to figure out where I was observing them from illustrates how difficult it can be to find the correct target.

. . .

The next day my division received orders to leave the Brittany peninsula and move east toward Orléans. I was told that Alex Graham had put me in for a Silver Star decoration for the church steeple action. And Alex was himself put up for his own Silver Star by Colonel Bixby. But the division's adjutant general, Lieutenant Colonel R. M. Connolly, arbitrarily reduced them to Bronze Stars, supposedly saying: "I'll be goddamned if I'll recommend a Silver Star for an artilleryman." On the Silver Star application sent in by Graham, Connolly had simply printed: "Bronze Star Award directed by C.G."

Nasty comments were made in my battalion about the adjutant's attitude and the fact that, as a rear echelon staff officer, he had never even seen action. We were offended: "We're getting shot at and this desk-jockey has the nerve to criticize us." Certainly, getting out of the steeple unhurt had been a close shave; another minute and I'd have been a goner. Our artillery battalion had taken causalities steadily since going into war and, in our parochial view, being an artilleryman was dangerous. But, looking back, I've changed my mind:

the divisional adjutant was right. Being a field artilleryman firing the howitzers several hundred yards behind the front lines was much less dangerous than being an infantryman or tanker on the front lines, a fact none of us considered. What Colonel Connolly failed to realize was that an artillery forward observer, like me (and Colonel Graham that particular day), was stationed at the front line, right alongside the infantry—a fact that would soon cost Dude Dent his life.

# 11

# "I AM GOING TO DIE"

**WE MOVED AT FULL THROTTLE** on a roadway south of Paris—from Caudan to Troyes via Vendôme, Orléans, and Sens. We had a minor fight at Vendôme, a fairly difficult one at Orléans, and, on August 21—my twenty-third birthday—another minor one at Sens. But our goal all along was to take Troyes, the capital of the Champagne region, where the Germans were entrenched and blocking the Third Army's progress to the east. As we got closer to Germany, the ferocity of their resistance seemed to intensify.

On August 22, the 94th Field Artillery Battalion went into position behind a small hill on the outskirts of Troyes. The plan was to attack the Germans the following day with a combat command consisting of two armored infantry companies and a tank company, all supported by artillery fire from my battalion. The challenge in this battle was the terrain: combat command had to cross a wide, open plain to get to Troyes, fully exposing it to enemy fire. The infantry and tankers would be reasonably protected in their armored half-tracks and tanks, but there were two groups that would be easy targets: infantry officers, who would ride in jeeps, and our forward observers, who would likewise be riding in unarmored vehicles. After what we had faced at Rennes with the German 88mm guns, this expanse of open ground between us and Troyes seemed especially dangerous to us forward observers. I wondered whose turn it would be.

And that's what brought Dude Dent and me together in a meeting the evening of August 22—an encounter that has always stayed in my mind. Looking concerned, Dent said he had a problem and he wanted my advice on how to handle it. I was puzzled as to why Dent was coming to me. He had joined the 94th about a year after me, and I almost never saw or spoke to him; he had always seemed somewhat aloof and unfriendly, and we hadn't bothered to get to know one another.

But once he told me what was on his mind, I felt the gravity of his predicament, as well as why he had chosen me as his confidant. Dent explained that it was his turn in the rotation—that he would be going out across the field in tomorrow's battle. Obviously, he was concerned for his own safety, but Dent explained that he had had a chilling premonition. "If I go on this attack," he said gravely and firmly, "I am going to die."

No ifs, ands, or buts: he was absolutely sure he would get killed.

Because, as the adjutant, I was constantly dealing with the top brass and had a better idea than most of which buttons to push in order to get a favorable response, he thought I might be able to get him out of his duty. Whether Dent would have done better choosing someone else to consult with I cannot say; all I know is that much as I wanted to help him, I failed to do so.

I thought of advising him to play sick and get a medical excuse from Doc Horowitz, our battalion surgeon, but I felt that Dent was an honorable person who would not countenance a ruse of that sort. It then came to me that his best bet was to talk to the man who made the forward observer assignments: Major Bob Parker. I held Parker in high regard and was sure he would do the best he could for Dude. Dent thanked me and went off to see Parker, to whom he described his premonition of death in the Troyes attack. Dent told me Parker listened to him carefully in a seriously sympathetic manner, but explained to Dude that he had no choice; the forward observer assignments were rotational and, as it was Dent's turn to go, he would be obliged to carry out his assignment.

Three of the 94th's forward observers took part in the attack on Troyes: by coincidence, all three had been at Colorado A&M in Fort Collins together. Lieutenant Wayne Seaman rode in his own tank with the tank company. He suffered only minor facial injuries from shell fragments that came through his tank turret. Lieutenant Albert Hoffman went with one of the infantry companies, driving in an unarmored jeep; miraculously, he made it across the plain unharmed. Dude Dent accompanied the second infantry company, also in an unarmored jeep, with its glass windshield laid flat over the jeep's hood.

I watched in growing apprehension from the sidelines. A sharp staccato burst reverberated across the expanse. Dent's premonition proved correct. Enemy machine-gun fire killed both him and his driver—they were barely halfway across the plain. What was particularly gruesome about this incident was that Dent was on his radio giving firing instructions when it happened, and we heard him scream as he was hit.

I couldn't help but feel like it was partially my fault. He had come to me in desperation, and yet I'd been unable to help him. All I'd done was give him some lame advice about going up the chain of command to Parker, whose hands, of course, were tied. As a commander, Parker could not make exceptions when it came to rotating duty assignments.

Then it suddenly dawned on me what I should have said to Dent.

Instead of asking Major Parker to relieve him of his assignment, he could have requested permission to ride across the plain in a tank instead of a jeep. Bullets would have bounced off a tank, and the odds are Dude might have made it across safely. But by the time that idea came to me, it was too late. Dude was gone. And I've always felt I missed a chance to save him.

Here it was again. The last emotion I expected from my service in the army. Guilt about people dying as a result of my actions. First, it was the two Germans in the hedgerows, now Dent. For some reason, Dent's death hit me especially hard. In all these years, hardly a day goes by that I don't think of Dude Dent.

We lost others at Troyes, besides Dent, but eventually we prevailed. The Germans had many casualties as well; and about one hundred men surrendered, which prompted grievous misbehavior on our part. I did not personally witness this—I was told after the fact. But apparently the hundred Germans who surrendered at Troyes were shot dead on the spot by our troops and left to rot by the roadside.

Everyone whispered about it—but, officially, nothing was ever said or done about this shameful action. It left me feeling uneasy. I was starting to realize that war brings out a certain madness in men—whether friend or foe—a madness that allows for the rule book to be thrown out the window. All bets are off out here.

As if that weren't grim enough, just as we were leaving Troyes and moving east, I came across my first burned-out half-track. It stood at a junction in the road, and there were four GIs in it, all burnt to an unrecognizable crisp. They'd probably been there for a few hours—victims of a German 88mm gun, no doubt. It was the most terrible sight I had ever witnessed. There was a driver, someone in the passenger seat, and two GIs in the personnel part of the half-track, looking like nothing I had ever seen before or since—roasted to black paper ghosts of their former selves. Ghastly.

As time went on, I saw more burnt bodies, plenty of them. But this was my first such sight, and it was a shock—etched in my memory, like that deep concern in Dude's eyes the night before he got shot. I'll never forget it.

. . .

Looking back, my memory receding, and having nothing other than my letters home as a record of my wartime experience, I find that only the most dramatic events have stayed vivid in my mind. The rest of my recollection—the stuff that happened in between—is more hazy than sharp focus.

We fought a great many fights during the war, large and small. But each battle has its own special identity in my memory. I have always thought of them as personal happenings. I viewed each as "belonging" to one or more of my Fourth Armored comrades or to me. Our first battle, the one above the Normandy coastline at Sainteny, belonged to George Powell and Bertil Nystrom, and to Herman Orsbon, who won the division's first Silver Star for his valor in this engagement. I identify the battle at Avranches with General McNair, who died in a tragic friendly-fire incident when his unit was bombed by our planes. But Avranches also reminds me of General Patton, whom I encountered standing and saluting us atop his jeep as we drove into town. The battle on the road to Bastogne was associated with Don Guild and Sherm McGrew, forward observers like me, who were responsible for capturing a large number of enemy soldiers during that engagement. And, of course, I identify the battle at Troyes with Dude Dent.

My own battles began on that country road (the brief lopsided encounter with those two poor unsuspecting Germans). They continued throughout Normandy and Brittany, culminating with the church-steeple incident at Caudan. But of all the battles I was in, the one we fought right after Troyes became, for me, the most melodramatic. It was the battle for Commercy.

This would be the first time I actually saw the enemy en masse, directly in front of me—not distant, as they had seemed from the church steeple. I would be more determined than ever to observe properly and serve to my highest potential in this battle. But I'd also succumb to sickening fright, followed by sudden elation and euphoric relief to have come through unscathed—an emotional roller coaster, to say the least, of a magnitude that I had never quite experienced before.

Commercy's strategic importance lay in the fact that it protected the Germans' positions in Metz and Nancy, major cities to our east, as well as the crossings they controlled on the

Moselle River. And the Moselle had to be crossed if we were to get to Germany.

When the action began, I was lying in a natural indent on a hilltop observation post outside of Commercy, accompanied by my radio operator and driver. We had managed to sneak sufficiently close for the enemy to be in plain sight in the valley in front of me—horse-drawn artillery, military vehicles, and marching infantry, moving on a road at the far side of the valley. Sitting ducks, or so I thought.

I felt completely secure that particular morning, the model of a Fort Sill graduate. I felt competent reading a map or aerial photo and determining where a target's position was. I was good at calculating ranges by sight, much as professional golfers do today, and I could transmit fire commands quickly, regardless of the pressure of combat. Lying belly-down on the earth that morning, binoculars perched to my eyes, I was in my element—doing what I did best and going with the grain, rather than against it. With eighteen howitzers at my beck-and-call, I felt powerful as all get-out. I went to work picking targets and radioing their coordinates to my battalion's fire control center.

I had to be sure to make each shot count, however. At Commercy, we had an unusual restriction: use ammunition sparingly. The Third Army was out of gas, and ammo wasn't reaching us; once we used up what we had, we'd be out of it entirely. So we were ordered to shoot at targets only when there were large numbers of troops or vehicles and to avoid shooting at single individuals or groups of two or three. In my case that day, I had plenty of choices. And I was close enough to see the results.

I watched as my fire bracketed the crossroads, causing enemy soldiers (who were not killed or wounded) to scramble. They must have called for help, because shortly thereafter fifteen or more Messerschmitt (ME) 109s soared above me, flying just above ground level. The ME 109 was considered to be Germany's finest attack plane; it was the one we dreaded most. Each had four machine guns that fired simultaneously. They made a terrible racket as they passed over me (oblivious to my presence, or I wouldn't be writing this) and began swooping to earth again and again to strafe our artillery battalions nestled behind me at the foot of the hill. I felt helpless. And suddenly scared out of my wits.

But, just after the air attack began, I sensed someone lying down next to me. I turned and saw, to my great surprise, that it was my buddy, Bill Lothian, the former Pan Am accountant and the commander of Battery C, whose fire I had been adjusting. His friendly grin in that moment felt like a lifesaver. He was a very close buddy, part of a foursome whose companionship I treasured. Bill's job was commanding the hundred officers and men trained to fire six self-propelled 105mm howitzers. This usually kept him behind the front lines, where he could rarely see the enemy.

On this particular day, however, he wanted to see the action with his own eyes, just like Graham had done in the church steeple. Having snuck up to my OP, he was able to see everything: the German army's armored vehicles, their horses and troops, their artillery batteries and their planes, swooping at almost ground height above us. While I lay there, terrified, Bill reveled in the action. Seeing the enemy for the first time since we entered combat, and finding it both refreshing and exciting, he shouted over the din with glee: "This is the great-est show on earth!"

I looked at him askance at first, but then couldn't help but grin. Both of us were unaware of the mayhem that was tak-ing place that very moment at the base of the hill behind us. As the air attack ended, Lothian left the hilltop and returned to his battery; I remained at the OP, directing fire for sever-al more hours until all signs of enemy forces finally disap-peared. I then went back down to find a scene of utter havoc.

Two artillery battalions, my own 94th and especially its sis-ter 66th, had been decimated. They had been deployed not far from each other at the base of the hill. Both were com-manded by able West Pointers—the 94th by Colonel Graham and the 66th by Colonel Neil Wallace. Each man knew he had to protect his unit from enemy artillery and mortar fire, but apparently only Graham thought that the Luftwaffe might be a serious problem. That's why Graham had gone to great lengths to defilade (i.e., conceal) the 94th properly, whereas the 66th was more exposed. Thus the Messerschmitts spot-ted the 66th and mauled it badly. But the 94th had also been impacted. Even though proper defilade had kept the 94th con-cealed from the planes, its artillery flashes had finally been pinpointed by enemy observers, and German artillery shells had hit Bill Walsh's Battery B, destroying a 105mm howitzer, killing Alex DuBovy, a gunner, and wounding several others.

One of the truly bleak roles I had as battalion adjutant was "graves registration"—when officers have to sign death re-ports of soldiers in their battalion who were killed in action. This is not an area in which you want to make a mistake. That means making damn sure that a burnt corpse is the man you think it is. So I had to kneel down next to what was left of

Alex DuBovy and check his blood-spattered dog tag. A grim assignment, to say the least.

But the damage to my battalion was nothing compared to the destruction at the 66th, where dead and wounded lay all over the place and equipment had been blown apart—a mess in spades. Six of its personnel died and fifty-seven were wounded and evacuated; its lack of defilade cost it ten percent of its strength, a heavy burden for its commander to bear. Among the men that Neil Wallace lost was his adjutant, so he didn't have anyone to do his "graves registration." Guess whom he asked for help?

Though I had to go through the grisly task of corpse identification six more times for our sister battalion, I didn't hold it against Wallace, nor did I lose respect for him. Wallace was well regarded by us junior artillery officers, and although I was a just-turned twenty-three-year-old and he was only thirty-three, I considered him to be a superior being whose knowledge and responsibilities went way beyond anything I could comprehend. In the desert he had exercised out in the open, by himself, swinging a large axe. When Colonel Bixby was promoted and left the division artillery command, Graham moved up and took over. When Graham was hurt and had to relinquish the post, Wallace was promoted to division artillery commander, proving that, professionally, both men did well. But the question remains in my mind: why wasn't the 66th properly camouflaged that day in Commercy?

There is no argument that being a battalion commander in the Fourth Armored Division as it spearheaded Patton's Third Army was no sinecure. Many commanders became overwhelmed by the pressure of moving at high speed while dealing with the Germans' superior fighting skills. Alex Graham, Bob Parker, Art West, and, most especially, Creighton "Abe" Abrams thrived under this pressure. But many others did not. The key, I think, was to figure out a good way to unleash your stress and manage the burden of being responsible for the lives of hundreds of soldiers under your command.

Abrams had a unique way of blowing off steam. His way of doing this frequently took place at night in castles we had taken over, where he and others would throw a party and drink rather heavily. Abe's particular pleasure came from firing his 45mm pistol at the walls, windows, mirrors, and chandeliers. It was an easy and—strange as it may seem—safe way to let off steam.

Finding a way to deal with stress was critical. When Graham was promoted to division artillery commander, Lloyd Powers took over his position as commander for the 94th Armored Field Artillery Battalion. All of a sudden he must have felt under a lot of pressure. I don't know exactly what happened, but after only thirty days on the job he was relieved of his command, purportedly suffering from stress-induced ill health. He was sent to a hospital in Nancy, and we never saw him again.

# 12

# THE SILENCE IS HARD
# ON MY EARS

**WITH THE THREE-DAY FIGHT** for Commercy over and the Third
Army out of gas, we had some days off—our first in months.
(To Patton's fury, what little gas was available at the front was
allotted at this time to the First Army rather than the Third
Army. British and American historians of World War II have
concluded that this was a strategic error, that if Patton had
been allowed to continue his advance, the war would have
ended much sooner than it did.) One of our rest days culmi-
nated in an outdoor movie, *Going My Way*, with Bing Crosby
and Barry Fitzgerald, which, for a moment, brought us back
to enchanting normalcy.

We stayed at Commercy for ten days waiting for gas (and
for the Third Army's rear to catch up). On September 8, 1944,
I wrote to my mother:

> We had a swell meal (a change from our K-rations) & then
> drank cognac brandy and talked until dawn. Then I went to

sleep and slept all day and all last night. The first time in 3 mos. I've been out of the range of the Jerry artillery & the silence was hard on my ears.

. . .

After Lloyd Powers left, we all wondered who'd be promoted. I was happy to find out that his job was awarded to newly promoted Lieutenant Colonel Bob Parker, who proved to be an inspired choice, working in tandem with his immediate superior, Alex Graham, now a full colonel and another leader who continued to awe me. I wrote a letter home that was an odd concoction of mundane details and a worshipful assessment of Graham:

> Hope to take a helmet sponge bath tonight. . . . The mail arrived. In it [were] Dad's delicious cookies. . . . Colonel Graham's dad had sent the Colonel a box of Hershey bars in the same mail, so we had a fine supper.
>
> Colonel Graham has got more guts than anyone I've ever seen. . . . He's a marvelous guy and is responsible for having saved many of our lives by his quick thinking and common sense.
>
> We are pretty far forward, ahead of all the rest, I think, and consequently take the brunt of the Germans' desperate resistance. . . . The war may be over to the shipyard workers and editors of Time, but it sure as hell isn't for us (i.e. bombed and strafed this afternoon by over 55 ME 109's).

Whenever I could get hold of a copy, I read *The Stars and Stripes* newspaper, which the army distributed to those of us in the field, and it mentioned that the media in the U.S., such as *Time* magazine, was reporting that the German forces were about ready to cave in. Nothing could have been further from the truth; the Germans battled fiercely for another eight months, and it wasn't until Hitler put a bullet in his brains that they surrendered, in May 1945. (I was even shot at by a Nazi SS soldier two days *after* VE Day.) How *Time* and other American media could have been so far off the mark baffles me. For the boots on the ground, there was still a lot left to this war, as we'd soon see.

What to us had been a lifesaving respite at Commercy was, in fact, a gift to the Germans in the way of time, which Patton and Wood fumed about. The generals were fully aware that the two key cities guarding the German frontier, Metz and Nancy, would be heavily fortified and that the bridges over the Moselle would be made impassable. The Moselle is not a wide river; it was formidable not because of its breadth, but because of the Germans' determination not to let us get across.

Eventually, our gas arrived, and we headed for a fight that would be grim and deadly. The goal of this fight was the capture of Arracourt, a small farming town that had to be taken before we could attack Nancy. The town was hard to get into, hard to stay in, and hard to move on from. Its name for me conjures up a harsh battle that went on for days and days, during which the Germans did their best to halt our eastward movement toward their homeland. It's the place where Lieutenant Colonel Creighton Abrams became famous throughout the army for his prowess in the field— and thank God for it, because, in military terms, Arracourt would prove crucial.

At Commercy we had been moving so fast that we caught the Germans, like the column of troops I fired on, by surprise. But this time they were entrenched and waiting for us, and prepared defenders always have the upper hand in battle. Attackers must outwit them with tactics or overpower them with strength. Lieutenant Colonel Abrams did both.

His great skill was getting his tankers to fire right away. For some reason, the tankers in our other tank battalions would get in their tanks, go out in the field, and then freeze and not fire the guns. Abrams's basic philosophy was: get those rounds out.

And Abrams had another philosophy that he used to expound at night to Tom Cooke, who was his favorite artillery liaison officer and, although junior in rank, a friend. Though Abrams hesitated to talk man-to-man to anyone in his own battalion, he got along well with Cooke, which allowed Cooke to speak frankly to the colonel. Cooke once overheard Abrams give a dreadful tongue-lashing to Captain Jimmie Leach, one of his company commanders. Cooke remonstrated with Abrams, saying: "You're not being fair with Leach, that was downright mean"—to which Abrams replied: "Tom, it's the only way to keep him going. Otherwise, Leach would be so scared of the enemy that he wouldn't function."

According to Cooke, all of the 37th Tank Battalion's company commanders infinitely preferred taking a licking from the enemy than facing Abrams's wrath, which is why we eventually prevailed at Arracourt, with strong support from the artillery.

Operating behind the lines, Bob Parker was close to flawless as an artilleryman and combat leader. On this deployment, he had chosen a two-story farmhouse on the southern edge of Arracourt as our battalion headquarters and fire control center. A large dirt courtyard was adjacent to it, with an outdoor latrine at the far edge and an uncovered cesspool at the center. The Arracourt farmhouse was a perfect model of my life "off" combat in the 94th: a place to socialize and play poker while a continuous battle went on outside. Parker put the three gun batteries into position in the field across the road from the farmhouse. I recall that on our first night it was very dark; some of us were in the farmhouse cellar playing poker by the light from our own generator when, suddenly, mortar shells began exploding all around us. Those of us in the cellar were reasonably safe, but those at the gun batteries were exposed and were hit. Our battalion suffered numerous casualties.

A few days later, it very nearly became my turn. I was at a small knoll not far from Arracourt, setting up an OP in the grass and getting ready to adjust fire on German troops dug in at Athienville, a town visible two-and-a-half miles to our north. Suddenly, hearing German voices close by, I fell flat to the ground—none too soon, as it turned out. A moment later, the grass above and around me was mown down by enemy machine-gun fire. Again, I don't know why I was spared. Was God protecting me? Was it just chance or fate?

I prayed a lot during the war. I had been fighting continuously for months, and I was a different person from the one who landed at Utah Beach: much more calloused and oblivious to the pain of others, most especially the enemy, and far more bloodthirsty and anxious to kill—yet I prayed. I prayed to alleviate my ever-present fear, often softly reciting to myself the 23rd Psalm. The anger and animosity that had built up in me would disappear while I was praying. Regretfully, it returned as soon as I stopped.

The Lord is my shepherd; I shall not want.

He maketh me to lie down in green pastures: he leadeth me beside the still waters.

He restoreth my soul: he leadeth me in the paths of righteousness for his name's sake.

Yea, though I walk through the valley of the shadow of death, I will fear no evil: for thou art with me; thy rod and thy staff they comfort me.

. . .

Either later that day or the next, I was joined by two unusually distinguished visitors: Generals John Wood and George Patton. They had come up behind me rather quietly, no aides or anyone else around them, and they took me by surprise. "Show me where we are, Lieutenant," General Wood said, proffering me his map case. I attempted to locate Arracourt on what seemed to me was a map of Europe, rather than of western France, but could not do so. Upset at myself, I showed the generals our location on my own map. They took up binoculars and looked around, thanked me, and left. This was the first time I had actually spoken to Patton, and I found him to be in soldierly working mode: no bluster or swagger, but rather thoughtful, quiet, and businesslike. The two times I had seen him previously, at the Garrison Theater in Devizes and standing by the roadside in Avranches, he was spurring us on and using all his magnetism to do so. I was to meet him twice again in the next few months, finding him unassuming and polite at the first meeting and kindly, inspiring, but then out-of-control at the last.

We spent the next weeks fighting in and out of Athienville, Bezange-la-Petite, Bathlemont, Lezey, and other little towns in Lorraine. The names have always remained in my memory, while the towns they stood for and the people in them have become a blank. But there is an image of these battles that stays in my mind: that of the Germans' terrifying airburst shells.

In the fall of 1944, while at Arracourt, the Germans started firing a new artillery shell that exploded about ten feet in the air, scattering metal fragments over a wide area—far more lethal and much noisier than the old-fashioned shell that exploded on the ground. These airburst shells did a lot of damage, and we ran fast for cover whenever we heard them. A bit later we came out with our own Posit artillery shell, which also exploded in mid-air and, we were told, created even more havoc than the Germans' shell. And so it goes, each technological development making lethal warfare ever more lethal.

# 13

# I STOP WRITING HOME

**I'VE ALWAYS BEEN A PERSON** who enjoyed letter writing, and I continued to do so even after we became combatants in July 1944. I'd write home at least once a week, because it helped me to feel I was still connected to the world of "normal"—not stranded out there, where at any given moment a man could go home in a body bag, maybe someone you'd just played poker with last night. One minute, your friend is laughing, getting drunk; next minute, he's a slab of meat.

Tomorrow's battle would take at least one more of us—that was guaranteed. We all dreaded tomorrow. That's another reason I wrote those letters home: to keep my mind off tomorrow.

By the fall of 1944, that dread had become all-consuming; it had leached into my bones. It meant more drinking. More praying. More denial. The numbness sapped away all ambition—and I stopped writing home.

I was aware that as an only child with a highly emotional mother, I was unnecessarily adding to her and my father's stress. But I had stopped caring, I guess. Their letters kept coming, however—and I was grateful to receive them.

I can't overstate the importance of opening a letter in a war zone. First of all, it indicated that our battalion had stopped long enough for the mail truck to actually catch up with us—which meant we were not, at that moment, deployed in battle, thank God. Second, someone invariably would be receiving a parcel with toffee, marshmallows, and other goodies from back home, and most of the soldiers in the 94th were pretty generous about sharing their treats.

News from home was cherished almost as much as the sweets, especially when it was good news. We heard, for example, that Charlie Gillens's wife had given birth to a baby girl, which meant cigars all round, slaps on the back, and some good-natured ribbing about what was in store for him. The ribbing went into overdrive in the case of John Kelly, when he received word from his WAC wife that she had just been promoted to captain, which meant she outranked him. We laughed until we cried, worried that he might literally have a stroke if she made major. It was great to laugh. The good-natured camaraderie is what kept us going. It meant we were there for each other, no matter what. As we rolled across Europe, these fellow soldiers had quietly become my family.

Meanwhile, back home, my real family, not having heard from me, began to get worried. My frightened mother begged my father to do something about it. My father, it turns out, happened to be acquainted with a United States senator, Sheridan Downey of California—so he decided to visit the district office. I have no idea what my dad said to the senator, but it obviously worked. Senator Downey must have contacted the army chief of staff, who relayed a message to a general in the field.

Next thing I knew, I was being ordered to report to Colonel Graham at Division Artillery Headquarters, which he'd been promoted to command. When I arrived, I found Graham and the division's adjutant general standing there looking grim.

"Boas," Colonel Graham said, "I have just received an order from the division commander. Goddamn it, Boas, write your folks a letter."

And so I did. In September, from Arracourt:

> You asked me to describe what the war is like, so here is a report. Today is our 75th day in contact with the enemy, 75 days of fighting without any real rest—except for one evening, when we saw an outdoor show. Normandy was a cinch compared to this. Ever since Troyes, the opposition has stiffened. The Krauts have poured it on since we crossed the Moselle. This letter will probably be stopped by some potbellied censor sitting in his warm, cozy office—but here's the picture. . . . The Krauts are a tough, intelligent bunch and they know how to fight.
>
> Since we started holding the line (instead of our usual advancing) we've been under a constant 24 hour a day shelling that jars your fillings loose. It really separates the men from the boys. Some of the men who used to talk big and act tough have cracked completely. I've seen some go absolutely insane and we have to strap them down.

"Battle rattle" was getting to the best of us. It affected our behavior, our ability to make smart choices. The following day, I'd be seeing this firsthand. As I sealed my letter in its enve-

lope, I was oblivious to the fact that tomorrow—the dreaded
tomorrow—we'd lose one of our finest men.

. . .

Weather conditions had turned horrendous. We'd been sleeping on the ground, ever since our deployment in France.
When it rained, this became miserable—freezing cold, deep,
wet, sticky mud everywhere. We had to sleep in soaked blan-
kets, with our clothes likewise thoroughly drenched. Our
combat boots were not made to resist this damp, so many of
us caught dangerous trench foot. Additionally, as we never
bathed or changed our clothes, we all had lice.

On November 12, 1944, First Lieutenant John Kelly decided that he'd had enough and that he was going to do something about it. Instead of lying in the mud again like the rest
of us, he decided that night to keep dry by sleeping in his light
forward observer tank. So off he went with his crew of four.
It seemed like a good idea at the time, but Kelly got careless.

He disregarded standing orders to post a guard and keep
his tank turret hatch closed. Thus, while he and his crew were
heating soup and coffee inside the tank, a German night pa-
trol sneaked into the woods and dropped a grenade into the
open turret, killing Kelly and badly wounding four others.

Whether "battle rattle" had contributed to his laxity in judgment, I cannot say. But one thing I know about John Kelly is
that he never bothered to disguise his fear, like the rest of us.
Long after the war, Parker told me how much Kelly had come
to hate being a forward observer, badly wanting to become a
battery officer.

Kelly's death devastated me. As a friend he was the best:
sympathetic, supportive, always willing to help, and a plea-

sure to be with because of his intelligence and sense of humor. A truly nice, considerate man. It took me a long time to get over him.

. . .

Between the need to replace our dead and our wounded, we had a constant influx of new personnel. As the battalion adjutant, it was my job to welcome them. One day at Arracourt, one of our mess trucks came up from the rear, and so did about a dozen new enlisted men, none of whom had ever been in combat. I gathered them by the side of the truck, where they were offered bread, jam, and coffee, and I started my welcoming speech. It was a short talk about acknowledging the fear that all of us felt, rather than denying it. I explained that, in my opinion, the best way to go about controlling fear was to jump into action, tackling the task at hand—to focus on doing something, rather than sitting idly and allowing the fear to fester.

But I hadn't gotten very far in my talk when a German shell came out of nowhere and hit just behind the truck! We all scattered, quite terrified. Amazingly, no one was hurt. If that shell had struck twenty feet to the left, it could have killed us all. Needless to say, the psychological damage from that close shave was fairly severe.

A few days later we moved several miles north and east to an area around Xanrey and Juvelize. Though the rain and ground conditions remained miserable, our sleeping conditions improved immeasurably when we happened upon some dry World War I tunnels, perfect for sleeping in. As irony would have it, we were now occupying tunnels dug by the Allies in 1914. Here we were, thirty years later, fighting the same damn war.

. . .

Amidst the hell that was the Saar Valley, several events occurred that greatly pleased me. The first was the issuance of waterproof combat boots called "shoepacs," which looked like something from L. L. Bean's current catalog and which kept our socks and feet blissfully warm and dry. I still recall the sheer joy of having permanently dry feet—it seemed hard to believe!

The second was being given the chance to have a two-day leave in Nancy (now in our possession) and to visit its showerhead. How I got there was the most fun of all: I flew to Nancy in a Piper Cub! We used these small single-engine prop planes for forward observation by air, which gave an unrivaled view of the enemy troop position. Flying at altitudes of 2,500 to 5,000 feet, they were extremely susceptible to enemy gunfire, however—and many of them were shot down.

Forward observation by plane was considered less reliable than measurements from the ground, where we had our charts and instruments. A pilot had to keep his hands on the controls; he couldn't be fussing with maps and azimuth rulers. So his coordinates were more like ballpark adjustments, using landmarks visible to all. Nonetheless, there's at least one instance—an ambush on a bridge—where a pilot forward observer almost certainly saved the battalion from annihilation.

Harley Merrick, the man who flew me to Nancy, was an outstanding pilot observer. Fearless in the face of enemy fire (shot down twice), he was one of the most effective fighters we had. Going overseas as a sergeant, he returned a highly decorated major. A loner and iconoclast by nature, with guarded opinions, he read voraciously. Merrick was modest, secure, and profane in a humorous and endearing way. As Harley gave his friendship sparingly, I treasured it all the more, and it has lasted a lifetime.

Spending time with Merrick in Nancy, I experienced the shock of being in an urban environment after more than a hundred days in the field. Slightly disoriented, I kept my focus on the only two buildings that really mattered: a billet for officers run by the army, where the beds had clean sheets and hot showers were available, and a building run by the Red Cross with a large officers' lounge for drinks and food. In other words, I couldn't have cared less about sightseeing—I was only interested in creature comforts, the most important of which was the hot shower (we were allotted about two or three minutes but always overstayed our time). A peculiar aspect of the billet was to be waited on by locker room attendants who happened to be German POWs—it was odd not to see them either in a prone position or with their hands over their heads.

To go from the muddy, inhospitable Saar to Nancy, the capital of Lorraine, in a toylike Piper Cub was a treat. And I found Harley's cheerfulness, laughter, friendliness, and gung-ho attitude both comforting and inspiring. The trip was a beneficial one, as it banished, short term, the fear-induced stress that was always with me when we battled. After flying back to my battalion, my fear was still present, but the break had calmed my mind a great deal. Unfortunately, as was always true at war, the calm wasn't destined to last long.

. . .

In early December, while we were fighting in and around Singling, I went to check on a stalled tank and its occupants and was standing by the roadside making notes when a jeep with three stars on its hood drove up and stopped. General Patton, who was sitting in the passenger seat, motioned me to come over, and I did so with what I believe was maximum dispatch, saluting and giving my name and rank. "Where is Twelfth Corps Headquarters, Lieutenant?" inquired General Patton.

Unfortunately, he was asking the wrong person. My duties never required me to know anything about where even my own division headquarters was located, much less the head-quarters of a higher level like corps. Nonetheless, I felt ex-tremely embarrassed to be obliged to say to my commanding general that I did not know. If Patton had gotten out of his jeep and slapped me, I wouldn't have blamed him. But I was very grateful for the fact that he was politeness itself: "Thank you, Lieutenant," he said and motioned his jeep to drive on.

I learned later that Patton was on his way to take a most extraordinary, drastic, and from my point of view, unfortunate action— namely to relieve Major General John S. Wood of the command of the Fourth Armored Division.

When the troops heard the news, we were flabbergasted. It was our view that the Fourth Armored was a great success story, and that the reason it had succeeded was *because* of General Wood. All of us who served with him felt he was the best possible commander alive, and we liked everything about him—his style, smile, verbiage, looks, his understanding of how to use armor, and his sympathetic manner toward all of us serving under him. No explanation was ever given to the troops, not even to the battalion commanders, and none of us understood why such an outstanding leader should have been removed.

I only learned what had transpired some forty years later, at a division reunion. Apparently, Wood, stressed and exhaust-ed after six bruising months of armored movement, found himself bristling under the command of a nonarmored type he did not respect: Major General Manton Eddy, a crony of General Eisenhower. Since the two were not able to work together, a choice had to be made. General Bradley, Patton's superior, must have approved Ike's preference, forcing Patton to remove Wood, not Eddy. The army, despite its rigor, was certainly not immune to cronyism and politics.

. . .

We ended our Saar Valley fight at Rimsdorf and were sent back south and west to Languimberg, a town about ten miles from Guébling, for a period of heavenly rest and maintenance. The division had been going almost nonstop for 146 days; now we did nothing for nine days straight, and it was bliss. I finally had time to update my folks:

> Should be in good shape for the attack on Germany . . .
> I hope it won't be too expensive for us—but the Germans are expected to fight to the last man. It'll seem like old times to go hunting the krauts once more—and this time should mark the finish.

Boy, was I optimistic. "This time" would ultimately mean four more months of hellish and unceasing combat.

# 14

# IT GETS TO THE BEST OF US

**FIGHTING IN THE DARK,** wet savagery of the Saar had been grim. But as we tried to move north in Belgium, with the Germans battling to hold every square foot of ground, the struggle became considerably worse. It began with an all-night ride to the outskirts of Arlon in subfreezing weather.

We did not know it at the time, but we were moving toward Hitler's last throw of the dice against the Allied forces in the west, with his top soldier, Field Marshal Gerd von Rundstedt, attacking in the Ardennes Forest with a huge new army—the so-called Ardennes Offensive or Battle of the Bulge, one of the most significant engagements of the war. In the moment, without the overview of history, we hadn't a clue about where we were headed. Nor did we know that the key to control of the Ardennes was Bastogne, exactly where we'd be deployed.

What I did know was that I'd never experienced such paralyzing cold as I did on that 150-mile ride from France to Belgium. The frigid air drove out all other thoughts. My thick gloves did not keep the cold out, and my fingers became stiff and unmovable. Everyone else had the same problem, but nevertheless morale that night was high, with lots of excited wisecracking, cheerful greetings, and exchange of gossip at the pit stops, everyone unusually alert and energetic. We knew, vaguely, that we were part of something big, but we had no specifics about what was happening. I don't recall sleeping during the long journey, although I must have dozed off at some point.

When we reached the outskirts of Arlon the next night, I knocked on the door of the first farmhouse I came across and was lucky to find a farmer and his wife who welcomed us and immediately set about providing my sergeant and me with a delicious supper of bread and cheese. They then proceeded to take us to the second floor and to a room with a comfortable double bed. Heaven, we thought—but there was one problem: the bed was occupied by their two young fast-asleep daughters. Without fuss or fanfare, the parents shook them awake and asked them to vacate the bed for us. The girls complied with nary a complaint. I was deeply touched by the generosity of this farmer and his wife. Not surprisingly, Arlon and my overnight stay with this hospitable family has long remained in my memory as a bright spot.

The comfort and warmth of Arlon quickly disappeared as we moved north toward the outskirts of Assenois, a town that we had to go through in order to get to Bastogne. The name Assenois still sends shivers of fear through me. We found that the Germans were well entrenched there, and they fought for all they were worth to stop us. Three days of grim combat ensued, with the Germans using mortars, grenades, snipers, mines, and machine guns to maximum effect. One of the casualties was my own jeep driver, Private First Class Draper Charles, the young soldier from the Deep South whom I had defended in a court-martial hearing during our desert training. His death hit me hard. Men were dying all around me. First Dude Dent, then John Kelly, now Charles.

While my battalion had a large number of casualties in the Ardennes, they were minuscule compared to those of our three infantry units. The infantry had the unenviable role of making the breakthrough into Assenois and the other towns we needed to move through, and it was they who took the brunt of the enemy's devastating weaponry. In an armored division the infantry battalions were officially known as "*armored* infantry battalions," but this was a misnomer if there ever was one, as they fought on foot, without protective armor of any sort; they had nothing to shield themselves from bullets, shells, grenades, or mines.

I wrote home while in the midst of the conflict:

> My heart bleeds for those poor guys. Armor fights in vehicles and there's a good deal of satisfaction to it—the risk seems worth taking. That element of satisfaction is almost completely lacking for the doughfeet.

The 53rd Armored Infantry Battalion, followed by the 37th Tank Battalion (Creighton Abrams's boys), eventually did break through and occupy Assenois—but, as with our occupation of Guébling in the Saar and Arracourt in Lorraine, we could not hold onto it. The Germans counterattacked and retook it. For three days, we were in and then out of Assenois; it truly was a monster. Finally, after much pain and grief, we routed the Germans and moved north toward Bastogne.

We had no contact with the Germans on our drive from Assenois to Bastogne, but three unusual events occurred—the first two, pleasant surprises; the third, grim and disturbing in the extreme. The first event was the arrival on Christmas Day of our mess trucks, providing us with all sorts of goodies we hadn't had for a long time—a welcome relief from our normal C ration and K ration fare. The second surprise took place in the early afternoon when, suddenly, the sky above us was filled with the roaring noise of a huge number of low-flying C-47 transports, which, to our utter astonishment, began parachuting supplies to us in the meadows adjacent to our road. Our column slowed a bit, and we raced from our vehicles to see what we could pick up. Imagine our delight at finding more packages of Christmas goodies awaiting us on the ground. We then saw them drop packages over Bastogne, providing what turned out to be much-needed food rations and medical supplies for the 101st Airborne Division trapped in the town. (The roadside drop to us was probably a spur-of-the-moment decision by the flight commander.)

Shortly thereafter, as we reached the edge of Bastogne, I was astonished to see a huge number of German bodies, at least a hundred or more, dumped in a pile by the roadside. The sight of them shocked me, as does its memory today, and I have often wondered how they came to be there. Had they fallen in the field of battle and then been gathered for burial? God forbid that this had been another massacre by us, like the one at Troyes. We'd heard that on the eastern front the Russians and Germans routinely executed their prisoners. But we Allies were supposed to follow "the rules." The rules of war . . . what an oxymoron!

Although we were moving slowly as we passed that pile of bodies, we did not stop, so I never learned how those enemy soldiers met their end. But the disquieting sight has left a permanent imprint in my mind.

. . .

Bastogne is a small town with narrow streets, difficult to negotiate with tanks and trucks. But somehow we managed to park all of our vehicles, eighteen howitzers included, on the streets in the southeast section of the town. My team found a spot for our half-track with its .50 caliber machine gun near a house we took over for our battalion headquarters, where I slept. We hadn't seen any Luftwaffe since they attacked us in Commercy in September, but on the night of December 27, 1944, they hit Bastogne with a vengeance. For some reason we were not ordered to shoot back, but instead told to find shelter as best we could.

Two nights later, on December 29, the Luftwaffe made a huge attack, dropping bombs and strafing us with machine-gun fire, in an effort to push us out of Bastogne. This time we were ordered to shoot back. I had had considerable machine-gun practice in the Mojave Desert and Texas, so, without blinking, I jumped onto my half-track and took over the machine gun, directly under where the Luftwaffe planes were swooping down at rooftop height, guns blazing. What possessed me to jump so readily into the line of fire? It did not feel like an act of courage at the time, I will tell you that, more like going on autopilot—doing what I was expected and had been trained to do.

I simply pulled the trigger and let the bullets rip. Our .50 caliber machine guns were designed to shoot at aircraft, so I had a solid chance of downing one of the bastards. The only problem was that they were firing right back at me. Each time one of the ME 109s passed overhead, it was like a deadly game of chicken, a fusillade of bullets in both directions. Fortunately, our return fire was forcing the German planes to fly at greater height, which reduced their strafing action a bit. But they were already taking a horrendous toll on us. I looked around and saw wounded men lying nearby who needed help badly, so I left my gun (it was taken over by a crew member) and gathered together a rescue party to move the wounded to the medics. The German planes continued directly above us, with their bombing and strafing, but somehow we got to Doc's medical site unscathed.

Looking back, the situation could not be described as anything short of terrifying. I had been so focused on firing at the enemy aircraft, however, and then moving my wounded brothers onto Doc Horowitz's stretchers, that my ever-present fear disappeared—an amazing feeling. If there was a plus side to combat, this was it: when I concentrated on the task at hand, be it firing a weapon or observing fire for our howitzers, I was almost always fear-free.

But this particular engagement, one of the most dangerous situations we had encountered, tested the best of us. When the attack ended and we all stood down, I learned that one of my old friends from our days in the desert and Texas had hidden himself in a basement rather than mounting a gunfight, as we had all been ordered to do. He was a fine officer, so I just can't bring myself to name him here. Everyone was shocked by his action. This was a comrade who exuded confidence in every situation and was the last one we expected to crack under pressure. But here it was again—"battle rattle" taking down the strongest among us. Mr. Nameless loved his family—maybe the thought of never having the chance to see them again got the better of him.

My friend was pretty much ostracized by many of my fellow officers after that incident. We all understood fear, but somehow or another most of us had figured out ways to handle it; in my own case, I prayed. I was saddened by my friend's behavior and felt alienated from him. I considered discontinuing our friendship because of my changed view of him. But I decided my sympathy and forgiveness outweighed my disappointment. Maybe Mr. Nameless had had a Dude Dent moment—a premonition in his gut to stay out of harm's way. Who was I to judge? Bob Parker apparently felt as I did, for no disciplinary action was ever taken.

But Parker did take an action later on that quite took me by surprise: he put me in for the Silver Star, which, this time, was *not* overturned.

# 15

# ICE CREAM IN BED,
# COURTESY OF PATTON

**IN EARLY JANUARY,** encamped outside of Clochimont, a small town in Luxembourg, we began nine more days of frenetic combat and rugged living. Our job was to keep the Arlon-Bastogne highway out of German hands, and to this end our division's 94th, 66th, and 22nd field artillery battalions collectively fired over 24,000 rounds. We sheltered as best we could from blistery, snowy weather in pup tents, as there was no housing nearby. As a result of all the firing and cold, we were exhausted and miserable. But then a dramatic change occurred—in mid-January, we moved to Rumelange (also in Luxembourg) in order to maintain equipment and rest for the troops.

Suddenly, we were living in friendly, warm houses, went to movies every night, and in general took it easy. Mail came flooding through. After all the vicissitudes of combat, Rumelange was sheer heaven.

Luxembourg City was only a few miles away, and I was amazed that they actually still made very decent ice cream there. Yet it's one thing to order your own ice cream; it's quite another thing to have a three-star general do the ordering and arrange to have it delivered to your bedside—something that was about to happen to Yours Truly, something I wouldn't have expected in my wildest dreams. But I'm getting ahead of my story.

Just as I thought things could not possibly get better, they did. We found out that our battalion would be allowed to send four officers to Paris, now in American hands. Colonel Parker, God bless him, selected Tom Cooke, Bill Walsh, Harley Merrick, and . . . *moi!* I got a weekend leave to visit Paris with three of my best friends, which proved to be an unforgettable experience.

When I'd visited the city ten years earlier with my mother and grandmother, we had stayed at the Hotel Majestic on Avenue Kléber. One of the nicer hotels in Paris, the Majestic had since been used by the German General Staff during their occupation and now was being tidied up for the Allied High Command. In 1945 we stayed at another upscale establishment: the Hôtel des Deux Mondes on Avenue de l'Opéra, now taken over by the American Red Cross for an officers' club.

Paris had changed quite a bit since I was there in 1935, when it seemed full of zip and beauty. It was cold, dark, and rainy this time; the boulevards were filled with mud, as the street cleaning department was not in operation. But Paris had been spared from bombing, thank God, so the monuments were all still standing. I had done some basic sightseeing at age thirteen, when I saw the Eiffel Tower and Les Invalides—and I wanted to see more. In 1945 our hotel was offering guided tours of the city, but when I suggested we take one, my companions rejected the idea out of hand. Walsh replied that he'd seen the Eiffel Tower on a postcard and that was enough for him. Thus, Paris, the storied Paris, eluded me this time.

There was no interest on anyone's part in exploring the Louvre, going to the symphony or opera, let alone visiting art galleries that carried works by Picasso or Matisse. We were far too pedestrian for that: our focus was strictly on bodily rest and relaxation. First order of business: hot baths (our first since England). It was bliss.

Next, we sauntered into the hotel's large and beautiful dining room in our clean uniforms, basking in the attention of our fellow army officers, whose eyes focused admiringly on our Fourth Armored patches. (The division was probably the most famous combatant outfit in the army at this period of time.)

On the streets there appeared to be more women than men (many of whom were still prisoners of war), and people seemed slightly unsure of themselves. After five years of German occupation, they were used to being bossed around, and they didn't quite know how to handle themselves now that the bosses had gone. The Métro subway was jammed; passengers looked overwhelmed. The most comfortable place by far was our hotel. Nonetheless, we toured the city, sampling sweets at attractive cafés and finding our way to "Pig Alley" (i.e., Place Pigalle) looking for women of the night. Back in 1935, Charlie Blair, a family friend who was my guide and sometimes chaperone in Paris, had primed my adolescent fantasies by introducing me to risqué French postcards. This time I wanted to experience the real thing.

We had heard a lot about Parisian nightlife from Colonel Graham, who had lived in France with the army for a couple of years before the war and had then taught French at West Point. He beguiled us with stories about a brothel called the House of Many Nations, which we tried, unsuccessfully, to find. Writing home about our weekend in Paris, I explained:

> We are organized into the 'No compris' club—as that is what we answer when the French ask us for tips or subway tickets, etc. In the Metro you are jam-packed up against one another. The inimitable Walsh organized the "Sly-Feelers Society," whose purpose, Walsh felt, was self-evident. He envisioned a competitive group who received points for seeing who could produce the loudest scream of anger.

Walsh triumphed when he pinched a girl in front of him and she, rightfully outraged, turned around and slapped Tom Cooke.

Tom was blameless, but Walsh was sly, and slyness was what our society was all about. Believe it or not, we felt proud of ourselves. Our juvenile behavior was due, I think, to combat-induced arrogance. But the Sly-Feelers were about to be shaken from their revelries with a stark reminder of the stakes of war.

Leaving the Métro that afternoon, we saw some women walking the boulevard with their eyes cast down, their hair completely shorn. Gazing at them curiously, I noticed they received scowls from French passersby and found out that these were women who had consorted with German soldiers when Paris was under Nazi control. I stared at them with fascination and pity, realizing how little I really knew about what had happened to Paris under Nazi occupation. I was completely unaware at the time that approximately 50,000 Parisian Jews had been sent to a French prison camp at Drancy and thence by boxcar to the gas chambers of Auschwitz.

. . .

When the weekend finally came to an end and we reluctantly returned to our unit, we were forced to tell stories for hours on end to our fellow soldiers, who were desperate for a vicarious morsel of what it must have felt like to visit Paris. As it turns out, we had done things that would be soon curtailed. A bit later, when other battalion officers went to Paris, the army declared nightclubs and cabarets to be off-limits.

I had gone to Paris with a cold, and it worsened because of the wet and freezing weather there. The Parisian restaurants and cafés had been like refrigerators, because there was no fuel for heating purposes. We were told that the orchestra musicians played concerts in their overcoats. I was coughing like crazy upon returning to duty, so I checked in with my friend Doc Horowitz, our highly regarded battalion surgeon, and asked him matter-of-factly for some cough medicine. Instead of giving it to me, he put his stethoscope to my chest, listened for a minute, and then sternly said: "You're sick, Boas. You're going to the hospital."

I knew there was no arguing with him—but I couldn't believe that after surviving unscathed through 180 days of shot and shell and outdoor living in all kinds of weather, I was suddenly being separated from my battalion. As I headed in an ambulance and checked into the hospital in Luxembourg City, I had no idea what an uncomfortable encounter was in store for me. In the bed directly opposite mine lay a young, badly wounded second lieutenant, a member of the Army Corps of

Engineers, who had arrived in Europe just a few weeks prior, on January 1, 1945. He could not have been more cheerful as he told me what had happened to him and his less severely wounded fellow engineering officer who lay in the bed next to him. It seems they had been working on a bridge when artillery fire, apparently from the American side rather than the German, came down on them, injuring them both. He had no clue that he was talking to an artilleryman, nor did I inform him of this fact. My expression turned to horror as it became clear to me that, because of the bridge's location, it was probably guns from my *own* division that had hit these two young engineers—maybe even from my own battalion.

At the time I was only vaguely aware of the persistent military problem known as "friendly fire." I first heard of it while in Normandy when General Lesley McNair was killed in a bombing raid by our own aircraft. But now, as I lay confined in the Luxembourg evacuation hospital, "friendly fire" was staring me right in the face.

Guilty feelings began to percolate in my gut, and they would only get worse. Later that day the lieutenant's leg was amputated, which made me more determined than ever not to bring up who might bear the responsibility for this tragedy. The lieutenant seemed better the next day, post-surgery, and was at the center of a most extraordinary event that began mid-morning.

Higher-ups, including the hospital's chaplain, chief medical officer, and chief nurse, began filtering into our ward without explanation. They stood silently and fidgeted nervously. It became evident why they were so jumpy a few minutes later, when the colonel in command of the hospital walked in, followed by General George S. Patton.

As my bed was next to the door (the room was rectangular and small, containing ten beds, five on each side), he approached me first, looking at me and seeing me quite undamaged. He said in his high voice: "What's the matter with you, boy?"

I said something like, "I have bronchitis, sir." My impression was that this answer disappointed him and that he would have preferred that I'd been wounded. I was afraid he might suddenly lash out and slap me, as he had done to the poor soldier who had been hospitalized in Sicily for "battle rattle."

Patton looked me over with narrow eyes and asked, "What outfit are you in, boy?"

"Fourth Armored Division, sir," I replied, and his attitude changed instantly. He put his hand on my shoulder, flashed me a big smile, and said, "Well, you deserve a rest—you've seen a lot." The Fourth Armored Division, which had been the spearhead of his army ever since Avranches and continued to be so until the war's end, was very close to his heart.

Patton then proceeded around our room, stopping at each bed until he got to the bed of the poor chap across the way from me, where something happened that I shall never forget. After learning the nature of the lieutenant's injury, which the hospital's CO whispered to him, and hearing about the exploit of this officer on a bridge under fire—the general didn't know that it had been friendly fire—he said: "Lieutenant, I'm going to award you the Silver Star." He then turned to his aide-de-camp, a close-to-fortyish and unmilitary-looking major who was wearing an army trench coat, and asked for a Silver Star.

The major, who was obviously under orders to carry decorations for just this sort of situation, started reaching in his trench coat pockets, first the left-hand pocket and then the right-hand one. A look of desperation suddenly appeared on his face as he began reaching into his jacket and trouser pockets. Everyone in the ward was literally holding their breath. Finally, the most dejected-looking major I have ever seen faced General Patton and said: "Sir, I don't have a Silver Star with me."

Enraged, Patton stood within an inch of the major's face and cursed him out for what seemed like an eternity, using the vilest profanity imaginable, while the hospital chaplain and nurses stood aghast. Even I, well aware of the general's legendary foul mouth, couldn't believe the tirade of curse words that were coming out of him. Then Patton's demeanor changed completely and became exceedingly gentle as he turned back to the wounded officer and said, "Is there anything you would like me to do for you, Lieutenant?"

The lieutenant spoke up and said, "I'd like some ice cream, sir."

Patton replied: "You will have it and your Silver Star within an hour, Lieutenant." With that, he and the unfortunate major left.

Within an hour a full colonel from Patton's staff arrived, looking very professional indeed—quite the opposite of the hapless major. He immediately pinned a Silver Star on the lieutenant's hospital gown, apologizing for it not having been available when General Patton was there, and saying that he had also brought ice cream—enough for everybody in the ward. Two soldiers came in and passed around huge bowls full of this delicious and unusual treat.

After I finished my bowl, I gazed at the young lieutenant, deep in thought. Though certainly nothing could come close to compensating him for the loss of a limb, I noticed that he seemed proud of his decoration. It assuaged my guilt a tad, even gave me a fleeting feeling of well-being. But the next day this feeling turned to ashes. My lieutenant friend died. He had been in Europe less than a month. It tormented me.

. . .

The doctors at the Luxembourg hospital felt I needed to go to a hospital in England to get rid of my bronchitis, but I was opposed to this, as I didn't want to leave my battalion. Thanks to Doc Horowitz's intervention, I was discharged and went back to the 94th for another ten days of indoor recuperation in Rumelange. I did much-needed adjutant's administrative work—awards, promotions, document signatures, preparing letters for the CO's signature, etc.—along with some extra-curricular work, which I described to my dad:

> I'm feeling fine again but still taking it easy. The jokers in the rear keep us well supplied with booze up at the front (officers only) and we receive a bottle of Scotch and sometimes an added bottle of champagne and cognac per month as a regular ration. . . . I usually fill my flask, which holds a pint, and then distribute the rest where it will do the most good.

I drank in the army to be part of the gang, but oddly now I was beginning to feel alienated from them. Though I had pushed hard to stay with my buddies and my beloved battalion instead of being sent to a hospital in England, in a letter to my mother I now expressed feelings quite to the contrary:

> It has been announced in the "Stars and Stripes" that leaves will be given soon to England. . . . I would gladly take one.

Think I'd like to spend my time . . . up in the Lake Country
with . . . Tom Cooke. Perhaps our Wren friends could come
along. . . . To get away from the war, the army . . . would be a
real treat. . . . For me a complete absence of a lot of fellow
soldiers is a prime requisite.

This shift from wanting to be with my fellow soldiers to
now wanting to be away from them marked a major psychological change. I was groping to see and plan for the future
and, as it turned out, was doing it badly. I knew I had to do
some forward thinking, and that my army life hampered doing this. But I was wrong—it wasn't army life that hindered
my planning, it was my post-combat emotional state.

This poor thinking on my part was a sign of things to come:
muddled decision-making about graduate school, career, and
Edna. At a time when I was thinking a lot about Edna, referring to her as "my Wren friend," instead of by name, in a letter to my family was only one of many indicators of confusion
and the beginning of increasing emotional instability. But I
mentioned "my Wren friend" often enough to concern my
father, who wrote me a nice, long letter extolling the virtues of
"home-grown products."

My father's pleas notwithstanding, I wish in retrospect that
in November 1945, at the end of my tour of duty, I had requested an army transfer to Paris instead of opting to return
to the United States. I think I would have enjoyed being with
the American community there and might have found it a
great place to unwind from the war, unlike my return to San
Francisco, which turned out to be nothing short of disastrous.

# 16

# THE MOTHERLAND

**WITH THE GERMAN BORDER** less than a hundred miles away, on February 22, 1945, the Fourth Armored Division left Luxembourg, moving into position to begin the attack on the enemy's homeland. My heart was now full of hatred for the Germans—all we wanted was to get this over with. But as our column rolled eastward, none of us had any idea of just how ferociously the German army was prepared to fight in defense of its motherland.

Unbeknownst to me, my letters home had become increasingly belligerent and bloodthirsty as the war progressed. Here's what I wrote to my father on February 18, 1945:

> Most of us who have been with it all the way have killed at least one German with a rifle or carbine at close range. Our battalion exec has killed dozens. Merrick, adjusting fire from his plane, probably wiped out well over a thousand. . . . It's a funny experience to look down your sights and see the kraut

drop. . . . I have no regrets for the small part I've played, and did what I had to do.

My attitude had changed drastically since July 1944, when Sergeant Plas and I shot the two Germans in Normandy. It would have been inconceivable at that time for me to have written home about seeing "the kraut drop." Here's what I wrote to my mother, one week later:

> This drive into Germany is like old times. We've been raising plenty of hell with the krauts. . . . We come upon Germans who are unaware of our presence, and I call for our artillery. Boy, oh boy—down it comes like thunder from Mars—round after round. . . . It's a real satisfaction to be on German soil. There is not going to be much left standing in this country, and that includes buildings, civilians and animals. Terrific destruction, and these babies asked for it!

Here's what I wrote to Goggy, my grandmother, on March 1:

> We are blowing everything we can lay our hands on sky high—and the destruction is beyond description . . . the people are destitute, no longer arrogant or swaggering Nazis, and are very unassuming and deprecatory. However, most of the fellows in my outfit hate them so much, that they'd just as soon shoot them as look at them.

The language and tone of my reports from the front lines shocked my family, as well as some family friends with whom my mother shared them. Especially disturbed was an old friend of my mother's (and mine) named Belle Moldovan, who had motored with us through parts of Europe in 1935. I lost track of Belle for almost forty years until I called her in 1975 while visiting her hometown of New York City. We got together and reestablished our relationship almost instantly—but she appeared surprised that I seemed "actually rather nice." When I pressed her to explain herself, Belle admitted she had been avoiding me all these years because my wartime letters were proof positive that I had become the mirror image of a virulent Nazi!

What triggered this murderous hostility—feelings that were *not* present when we first entered combat—I've never been quite able to put my finger on. Clearly, fear was the inciter. But how and why does the fear go on to beget savagery?

Thinking back and trying to make sense of it today, I know there was a good deal of macho bravado in these letters. I don't remember my comrades demonstrating such hatred, and most likely I was showing off in order to prove that, as an only child, raised in a matriarchy of two dominating women and an acquiescent father, I was now a man among men. I certainly loathed (and feared) the Nazis and knew more than most of my contemporaries about them, but I was still clueless about the Holocaust—all of us were. While that was about to change, in early 1945 we knew nothing of the horrific extermination campaign against European Jews. Had I known that Nazi death squads had already shot and killed over 1,00,000 unarmed Eastern European Jews, or that 3,000,000 were gassed to death in Polish killing centers, or that 800,000 more Jews died of disease and starvation while locked up in ghettos, my feelings in 1945 would have been even more vicious—though it's hard to imagine being more hateful than I already was. The fact is that I had become a cold-blooded killer in the line of duty or—as the army might have called me—a model soldier.

. . .

When my battalion went into firing position not far from Obersgegen, Germany, the Wehrmacht soldiers were well dug in beyond this town in hilly, wooded country. I had been assigned as lead forward observer, along with two others helping to support the attacking 51st Armored Infantry Battalion. A grueling battle, it would take us five days to advance less than fifty miles into Germany.

Thankfully, I was being deployed this time with the "cavalry"—that is, I was able to ride and do my forward observation in an armored half-track, rather than my jeep. I was thrilled; the cavalry was so completely different from my own battalion, whose routine was "set the guns down and shoot." Cavalrymen, in contrast, never stopped, continuously gallivanting hither and yon, which made for excitement and high spirits.

Excitement, stimulation, novelty—this is what I now craved. A combat pro ready for action, I had become callous to death, even our own losses. I now expected them as daily occurrences, so I rarely gave it more than a second thought when I heard someone in my battalion had been killed (unless it was a close friend like Kelly). Getting killed was to be expected, I felt—so, move on.

We'd all be moving on soon enough, at least the survivors would. We would soon pack up our duffels and be expected to go home and return to our ordinary pre-war lives. It was a transition I could not even fathom. In a letter to my grandmother, I wrote:

> It's a funny thing, Goggy, but I've just about given up trying
> to do any serious thinking anymore. When I was in college,
> it seemed awfully simple to reach a conclusion on almost
> any question, but when I think back to those Commonwealth

Club debates, I realize that I no more knew what I was talking about than the man in the moon.

Writing to my grandmother that I had "just about given up ... serious thinking," I was actually describing a psychological problem that was to plague me for years to come: the inability to assess and make sensible decisions. It's not a wound that leaves a visible scar, not like the loss of a limb. But the havoc that war wreaks on your internal wiring is no joke. My brain may have been okay, structurally; the problem was that I couldn't use it.

As we moved towards Ohrdruf, I started to get reckless and pushed my luck to the limit, making me an easy target for the enemy at Üdersdorf and at Heimboldshausen. On both occasions, I was extraordinarily fortunate. The Germans, who had been ordered to fight for every square inch of their soil, were making an all-out last stand. Slugging it out with them was definitely no fun; they were prepared to die and to take as many of us as possible with them in the process. As part of this final hurrah, the Nazi government had formed a new militia called the Volkssturm, which included males as young as sixteen and as old as sixty. The Volkssturm was a motley group, not well trained, but they fought hard and proved quite dangerous.

By late afternoon of March 6, the 94th reached Üders-dorf, cleared it of enemy infantry, and proceeded to set up headquarters in the town inn, better known as a *Gasthaus*. As enemy firing appeared to cease and darkness fell, a poker game began in the HQ. The players included Jack Merriam, now the CO of Headquarters Battery, and me. About ninety minutes later, Jack and I both decided to go outside and get some fresh air. No sooner had we cleared the doorway and entered a courtyard than we found ourselves enveloped in a screaming meemie attack. We scrambled to back up against the wall adjacent to the door, as did three enlisted men who had been standing outside, and we held our collective breath, knowing that the meemies could land anywhere. Their noise was deafening, and the wait seemed interminable. Eventually the cluster of six shells hit, one of them directly in front of us. It felled—but didn't kill—Jack.

The attack had caught us by surprise, and everyone scrambled to take up defensive positions. Medics picked up the injured men, and Doc Horowitz told me later that Jack, who had been standing next to me, had a serious leg wound. The Gasthaus roof and two of its rooms were destroyed, and five enlisted men (Walter Zelinski, Eiden Rorem, George Wood, Paul Emmett, and Francis O'Connor) were wounded. I found out later that they, along with Jack, were evacuated to hospitals in England.

Yet in the thick of battle, it was rifles out and back to business. I only thought fleetingly about how lucky I was to have had the Nebelwerfers miss me. At this high-stakes moment, I felt neither fear nor rage, but only an automatic sense of doing my duty. It was as if a voice inside me spoke: "Get to your half-track, Boas. We'll be moving out."

And, sure enough, that was precisely the next order that came down from Parker.

. . .

Merriam's sudden evacuation caused a shifting of jobs. Tom Cooke took over his job as the commanding officer of Headquarters Battery and I took over Tom's job as battalion liaison officer. As an artillery battalion, we usually were in support of one battalion at a time, either infantry or tank. Whichever it might be, our liaison officer would work with the tank or infantry battalion commander and his staff to supply fire where they wanted it. Once a fire plan had been decided on, forward observers would go wherever they were needed. The 94th probably spent more time in support of the 37th (Creighton Abrams's Tank Battalion) than any other unit; we were a good team, and we began to move efficiently from town to town.

I wrote to my father on March 9, 1945:

> It's a great thrill to be out of the stagnant lines and rolling across enemy territory, smashing the opposition as you go. When we take a town, we really shove the civilians around— and it is a pleasure—oh Boy! The only things the krauts react to are strong-arm tactics, and these are applied with a will. They're a mighty scared bunch these days . . . and the white flags hang from all the windows—hot dawg!

On the same date, I wrote my mother:

> We're kicking the hell out of these krauts. . . . I wish I spoke German the way you and Goggy do. I think my invective would be more appreciated, but by golly, they sure as heck understand a gunpoint.

Both of those letters were written on the stationary of the local Bürgermeister (mayor), whose offices we regularly commandeered as we captured villages. I had made myself right at home at his fancy desk, helping myself to a pen and paper. Several days later, I wrote my father from another town:

> As liaison officer they've really set me up in style . . . I have a very large room overlooking the square . . . filled with all kinds

of Nazi craperoo—Hitler philosophy, herrenvolk doctrine, files on the racial history of the families in the town, etc.

Three days later, on March 17, we were finally able to cross the Rhine, but German resistance was still surprisingly strong. It was difficult for those of us in the field to judge enemy troop morale, but an incident the following day demonstrated its decline to me in graphic fashion.

I was ordered to inspect a just-deserted battlefield on the eastern side of the Rhine, which I did, accompanied by my jeep driver. The field was pockmarked with shell holes and appeared totally devoid of humans. We dismounted and were walking around when we came upon an especially large shell crater. When we reached its edge and peered over it we saw six German soldiers, fully armed, staring at us from the crater's bottom. They could easily have killed us with no one the wiser, and just a few weeks earlier they surely would have done so. But now, upon seeing just the two of us, they instantly raised their hands in willing surrender and, after climbing out of the crater, with only the eight of us on the entire empty battlefield, they meekly gave up their arms and followed us into captivity. (How I wish this could have happened with those two Germans in the Normandy hedgerows.) No lives were lost. It seemed strangely civilized.

. . .

On March 25 we attempted to cross the Main River at Hanau. But we ran into trouble in the dark, thickly wooded forest through which we moved as we made our way to the bridgehead. The combat command I was in, consisting of three battalions of infantry, tanks, and artillery—about 1,500 troops in all—started out about 7 p.m., expecting to arrive at 10 p.m.

Instead, at 11 p.m. we were lost and still deep in the forest. I checked my map and aerial photos and concluded we were going around in a circle, and so informed Bob Parker, who in turn informed the West Point colonel in charge of the combat command that was leading us. The colonel changed his direction, and we staggered into our destination on the west side of the Main at about 2 a.m.

Our goal was to capture the only remaining bridge over the Main River, and at 5 a.m. all hell broke loose from German forces on the eastern side in the vicinity of Hanau. The battle for Hanau was a bloody one, and I always felt it was won by one man, a 94th tank forward observer named Lieutenant Sherman ("Sherm") McGrew, who was a relaxed, fun-loving friend of mine with a good sense of humor, and, like Don Guild, Harley Merrick, and Billy Wood, he also had a great deal of courage.

Though Sherm had been in lots of tough fights (and I never recall him complaining about any of them), this one at Hanau was the worst by far. The Germans put a large amount of artillery, mortar, and rifle fire on the bridge to keep us off, and their ME 109 aircraft bombed and strafed it. Our own infantry pulled back from the bridgehead in the face of this fire, but McGrew, Sergeant Richard Lane, and their tank stayed put—an easy target out there all alone—while he continued to give our fire center the coordinates to hit the enemy. And we eventually did hit them hard, forcing them to retreat and leave us in control of the bridge. It's a miracle that Sherm survived; for their bravery he and Lane were awarded Silver Stars, which, without question, they had justly earned.

One week later, I, too, would find myself in a hairy situation. My fight took place in a tiny, nondescript town in western

Germany called Heimboldshausen, midway between Fulda and Eisenach, which we reached six days after leaving Hanau. It had been slow going—only ten miles a day—because of enemy infantry opposition in towns we had to go through, such as Schlitz and Helmes, but also because of strafing on the roads from a suddenly reinvigorated Luftwaffe. German troops were dug in and around Heimboldshausen, and we were moving slowly up a hillside road toward the town when I found I had to relieve myself, as did Bill Lothian, who was in his jeep nearby. We dismounted from our vehicles and walked to the side of the road to urinate, armed with our carbines and pistols.

I didn't even have a chance to unzip my fly before we noticed two armed German soldiers in some bushes thirty feet below us, both with panzerfausts (anti-tank weapons much like our bazookas), obviously lying in wait. By the time they turned, I was already poised to open fire with my Walther P38 pistol—ironically, a standard German army weapon. Lothian drew his weapon, too. We fired four rounds, shooting them both—very likely preventing several of our tanks from being destroyed and probably saving some lives. Lothian turned to me in stunned silence. As a battery commander, he stayed with the guns and was rarely on the front lines. That's what had prompted him to sneak forward to my OP that time at Commercy and declare it "the greatest show on earth." But the greatest show had suddenly become very gritty.

The action prompted Bob Parker, now our colonel, to put us up for Silver Star commendations. Parker had been hoping for a chance to award Lothian, who was a top-notch soldier but rarely in a position for a Silver Star citation, which requires direct engagement with the enemy.

I was happy for Bill, but I hardly felt heroic about what I had done—quite the opposite, in fact. Sherm McGrew had deliberately stuck his neck out to help vanquish the enemy. He had remained exposed in his forward position rather than retreat, knowingly risking his life for the sake of the battalion. Our incident, on the other hand, was inadvertent—when the battle instincts kicked in and we drew our weapons, it was about self-preservation, not heroics. And I still remember the terrible sound that came from the mouth of the first German I hit. He was crying out in agonizing pain; I will never forget it.

The essence of the situation—the reason they're dead and we're still alive—is simply that we saw them before they saw us. It was just like that encounter in Normandy on my first day in combat. In fact, despite increasing jingoism in my letters, I felt no pride in relation to my behavior in this encounter, only sadness, which bolsters my own suspicion about the tone of my correspondence home: that it was merely belicose bluster to cover the incessant fear that plagued my every waking minute.

. . .

As we cruised along the autobahn one week later, heading north toward Gotha, we were expecting nothing but a joy ride—feeling the spring breeze and dreaming of our imminent discharge. Suddenly, the bridge ahead of us got blown to smithereens—booby-trapped by the Germans—and all hell broke loose. It was an ambush.

I felt a sudden rush of adrenaline—but, as I kicked into action, I was no longer afraid. Whether by virtue of my training or simply survival instinct, I found myself on autopilot. First thought: take cover, which meant diving under my jeep. I kept my head down and steeled myself. Wincing as the artillery bombardment began, I calculated they had four 88mm guns, two on each side. I watched helplessly as the armor-piercing fifty-pound shells pummeled the ground around our column like miniature earthquakes. It took only one miss before the Germans adjusted their targeting and started picking off our tanks like flies. Then a dozen panzers rolled out from their camouflaged positions. We were sitting ducks.

Was it really going to end like this? After everything we'd been through? This was supposed to be the homestretch. And then I heard a sound I will never forget—the most beautiful sound imaginable. The distant whir of a Piper Cub coming from above. It was Lieutenant Ed Smith—a forward observer operating from a propeller plane. From his perch in the sky, Smith had a perfect view of the entire battlefield, including the muzzle flashes of the German guns, which was all he needed to direct the fire back.

Sure enough, our 105mm mobile howitzers began return-ing fire and the momentum of the battle shifted in an instant. I felt a mixture of relief and euphoria. Our big guns saved the day, and I was damn proud to be an artilleryman.

. . .

The next morning—April 4, 1945—it became evident why the Germans did not want us to cross that bridge. This was the day that Parker and I stumbled upon chilling evidence of Nazi crimes against humanity outside the town of Ohrdruf. Walk-ing into the gated compound, we were confronted by scores upon scores of gaunt, skeletal bodies, recently murdered by shots to the head or beaten to death, stacked one on top of the other. Most of the corpses were identified by Jewish stars.

I approached the pile in abject horror. This was a watershed moment, both for me and for our nation. Up until this point, there had been an abstract quality to Nazi evil. Certainly, there was the rhetoric: the tirades against Jews, the deportations, the stories I had heard. But seeing the horror up-close, feeling the shock—it suddenly concretized the most diabolical extreme of what we humans are capable. I couldn't believe that the animals that had done this and I were the same species. Hitler was a monster.

As Parker and I surveyed the grounds, we came across a few living inmates who had hidden as the guards were evacuating the able-bodied prisoners. Apparently, any prisoner who could walk had been force-marched about forty miles to the larger Buchenwald, of which Ohrdruf was a satellite camp. The rest of the prisoners had been finished off with gunshots to the head and piled up in the yard, except these survivors who had managed to hide. One of the surviving inmates who spoke French told me that an American flyer from Berkeley, California, was among those in the courtyard stack. I could hardly believe what I was hearing—someone from my own backyard? I wondered if he was Jewish, as I hurried back to the pile to try and identify him. The body in question wore clothes similar to the others (but no Jewish star), and although his face did look American somehow, or so I thought, there were no dog tags, so I was unable to make a positive identification.

Glancing over the expanse to the villa across the street, from which we had first spotted the camp, I couldn't understand how a wealthy German family could actually own a home that overlooked this grisly horror-scape. We had learned from the servants that the owner was the local head of IG Farben. (That was the company that manufactured the gas used in the gas chambers—though I didn't know it at the time.)

It would take me a very long time to make peace with this ghastly experience. Ohrdruf was among the first places I would seek to revisit long after the war—along with Utah Beach and the bell tower at Caudan. Many years later, I would need to come back to these places to help heal the fissures they had created in my heart and my mind.

Shortly after our discovery of the camp, six of the SS camp guards were captured by enlisted men in one of our gun batteries. The men, some of whom were Jewish, requested permission to "take care of" the guards while escorting them to a POW camp: in other words—kill them. Parker, a man of consistently firm character, denied the request and saw to it that the SS murderers became proper POWs.

Upon our finding of the concentration camp, Colonel Parker had immediately sent word up the chain of command, and on April 12, the brass rolled into town—not just General Patton with the three stars on his helmet, but Four-Star General Omar Bradley and Five-Star General Dwight Eisenhower, as well. (Our coming across the Ohrdruf camp had been a monumental discovery.)

Though they'd received intelligence reports throughout the war of Nazi atrocities, the generals simply had to see the situation with their own eyes. It was just one week after Parker and I had first stumbled upon the brutal scene, and while the corpses had been sprinkled with lime to hasten decomposition and mitigate odor, eight days without burial had made the stench overwhelming.

According to one eyewitness, Eisenhower was so disgusted that he vomited on the spot, as did Patton, who then proceed-

THE MOTHERLAND  ★  191

ed to wipe his mouth and climb onto his jeep, where he went into a diatribe about tearing up the Geneva Convention and getting our just revenge on these SOBs. In his outrage and indignation, Patton ordered the Bürgermeister of the town of Ohrdruf and his wife to come and inspect the concentration camp personally. The mayor had claimed that Ohrdruf's citizenry was unaware of its existence. But shortly after viewing the camp, the Bürgermeister and his wife both committed suicide.

On April 15, Patton toured a larger and more horrific site: Buchenwald, the main camp, of which Ohrdruf was a subsidiary. This is how he described it in a letter to Eisenhower, written that very day:

> We have found at a place four miles north of WEIMAR a similar camp, only much worse. The normal population was 25,000, and they died at the rate of about a hundred a day. The burning arrangements, according to General Gay and Colonel Codman who visited it yesterday, were far superior to those they had at OHRDRUF.
>
> I told the press to go up there and see it, and then write as much about it as they could. I also called General Bradley last night and suggested that you send selected individuals from the upper strata of the press to look at it, so that you can build another page of the necessary evidence as to the brutality of the Germans.

Among the press corps who accompanied General Patton was photographer Margaret Bourke-White on assignment for *Life* magazine. By month's end the entire world would see the gruesome extent of Nazi war crimes against humanity. Patton was so appalled that he forced not just the Bürgermeister this time, but the entire population of the town to walk through the Buchenwald concentration camp—all 1,500 of them. It took two days for the Weimar residents to file through the camp. The German civilians had to march five miles up a steep hill, escorted by armed American soldiers. They must have been aware on some level of what was happening in the camp—the smell of burning flesh alone can carry for miles. But seeing it up-close was an experience that they (and I) would never forget.

# 17

# I SLEEP IN HITLER'S BED

**IN THE DISTURBING WEEK** after our discovery of Ohrdruf, I wrote a particularly vicious letter home:

> I'm afraid killing has become a little too natural to all of us—like eating or sleeping. In all these towns we find hundreds of Russian and Polish slave laborers . . . used as domestics, farm and factory laborers, and in Wehrmacht bordellos.
>
> Out at the racetrack there was an 18 yr old kraut gal who spoke English. When we asked her how the Germans could perform such atrocities, she said it wasn't the Germans but the SS (Nazi Schutzstaffel)—to which we replied: "Baloney, sister." At the paddock, the trainers were reluctant to saddle up the horses for us. My driver clubbed the first one he could reach over the noggin with the butt of his rifle, and the horses were then speedily saddled. That's the only language these bastards understand—we treat them pretty rough. . . .
>
> Hope this will be over soon.

We all wanted it to end—desperately. The 94th left Schwabhausen on April 12, 1945, moving east on the autobahn to meet up with the Russians in Czechoslovakia. All of a sudden, the column came to a halt for no apparent reason. There was nothing blocking the roadway, and certainly no enemy to be seen. Wondering what was happening, I began noticing soldiers jumping out of their vehicles and huddling around their radio sets, listening intently to the broadcast. The end of the war, I wondered—has Hitler surrendered?

I rushed to join one of the huddles and listened eagerly. Then my face dropped: Franklin Delano Roosevelt had suffered a massive cerebral hemorrhage—America's longest-serving president, who had led the nation through the Great Depression and World War II, was dead.

Roosevelt had been confined to a wheelchair since 1921, when he contracted polio; and by age sixty-three his health had been in decline for some time. But still, it came as a complete shock to me.

I idolized FDR. I had probably listened to every speech that he had ever made. I remember how thrilled I was when he said that we were going to have to build an air force of 50,000 planes, and that it was high time we assumed new international responsibilities. I felt completely aligned with FDR's politics, so much so that I even had a beautiful bronze plaque of him in my bedroom, given to me by the father of a friend who owned a foundry. Hearing that he was gone was unbearable to me.

Hoping to keep my emotions in check, I walked over to the mess truck for the comfort of some hot coffee. Sergeant Bill Taylor, our battalion's mess sergeant, was in charge of the truck. I was fond of Taylor. Intelligent, good-humored, and hard-working, he did an outstanding job producing highly edible food for all 500 of us, doing so under often dreadful and dangerous conditions and with only mediocre ingredients.

As Bill poured himself a cup of coffee and came over to join me, I was happy to have someone to commiserate with about FDR. Then he blurted out suddenly: "Boy, am I glad that dirty son of a bitch is finally dead!"

It felt like a slap in the face. I was so naive that it didn't occur to me that someone could have a political viewpoint diametrically opposed to my own. For me, a political liberal like my mother, FDR was heaven-sent; things were so black and white for me that I couldn't fathom how anyone could hate him. I had known Bill Taylor, who was from McKeesport, Pennsylvania, since our days in the Mojave Desert, and liked him immensely, but clearly never realized that he must have been politically conservative—and FDR's broad-minded, liberal policies infuriated conservatives of all stripes.

I'm somewhat ashamed to admit this but, while Taylor and I continued to serve together for another six months, I never forgave or spoke to him again.

. . .

As we moved along heading for Bayreuth, which was about ninety miles away, our column came to another halt along the autobahn. Something up ahead was blocking the way. A group of German boys materialized from a field next to the road and approached us, asking for "Schokoladen und zigaretten bitte." I would have guessed they were in their midteens, although I saw one or two who seemed much younger. They were wearing what appeared to be a different sort of ill-fitting uniform from the standard trimly fitting Wehrmacht uniform. I think we knew it was the Volkssturm uniform, but at this point the Volkssturm meant a youth group to us, not a military force that we should be concerned about.

As we had lots of chocolate and plenty of cigarettes, we gave them a generous amount of each. My recollection is that they didn't say "thank you," but simply turned and went back into the field. We paid no more attention to them, although we should have. Suddenly, we found ourselves being fired upon by rifles and panzerfausts (the kids had dropped these weapons in the field's tall grass before approaching us)!

Along with the men around me, I returned fire. Outgunning the ragtag militia three to one with our machine guns, carbines, and pistols, we quickly overwhelmed them—and the field fell silent. We had just shot down a bunch of kids, but there'd been no choice: these teenagers had become killers. Their primary target was a couple of light tanks and their crew a few vehicles forward from mine in the column, and they succeeded. Two of our men lay dead, three others wounded, two tanks destroyed. Why? For what? It was enough to make your head spin.

I could not believe that those kids had actually sacrificed their young lives out of some lingering loyalty to a fanatical madman, who, within a matter of weeks, would be dead by his own hand. One minute they're acting like textbook teenagers, the next, they're assassins. And kamikazes, no less! Surely, they realized they wouldn't stand a chance in the gunfight. It seemed so pointless.

Lord, I thought, when will this end?

. . .

On April 23 we went through the smoking ruins of Walden-burg, a Nazi forced labor camp containing live Jewish inmates. There were thousands of them who had worked as forced laborers in a nearby munitions factory. The dirtiest-looking bunch we'd seen to date, they wore long striped pajamas that looked like San Quentin garb of olden times; their heads were shaved, and each had a big yellow star on his or her back. This is how I described the scene in a letter home:

> They were unlike any other prisoners I've seen to date, it's hard to describe … as one of the boys put it: "they look shifty." They looked like a bunch of rats—don't look you in the eye—an awful sight.

But one group of women did look me in the eye, as I got out of my jeep and walked through the fenced enclosure. Women outnumbered men by fifty to one at this camp, and this particular group seemed especially excited to see me. One of them stared, pointing her index finger and asking in German: "Judisch?"

I recognized the German word for "Jewish" and was stunned that she had immediately spotted me as a Jew. I guess she must have seen something distinctly Semitic about my face (certainly, my nose!). And clearly ethnic radars were more finely tuned here in Germany, where institutionalized anti-Semitism had been the doctrine of state for over a decade. I thought back to that German lieutenant we had captured in Normandy who snarled at me with his steely eyes. I'll bet he had seen it, too.

But, unlike that Nazi POW who had regarded me with disdain and hatred, these women seemed to be in awe of me. It occurred to me that they were entirely unaccustomed to seeing a Jew who was obviously free and not utterly despised, a non-member of society. But it was more than that; they were staring at my uniform and taking in my rank. It must have been a first for them and totally inconceivable—a Jewish officer.

. . .

As we arrived on April 24 in Ramsenthal, a small town just outside of Bayreuth, no one in my outfit knew where we were headed. A few days earlier we had been outside of Chemnitz, close to the Czech border, and further east than any other American unit. We were expecting to join up with the Russians, but apparently the higher-ups had other plans for us. I hypothesized that we might be sent south toward Munich, or southeast toward Vienna, or due east toward Prague. But no one knew for sure, and until a decision was made, we had little to do except rest and enjoy ourselves.

With that in mind Lieutenant Les Davis, a fellow forward observer, and I headed for Bayreuth in the late afternoon to visit its famous opera house (the *Festspielhaus*) and Villa Wahnfried, the home of Richard Wagner, whose music had been appropriated by the Third Reich. Hitler regarded Wagner as his favorite composer; they also shared political views—Wagner was a raging anti-Semite.

Wagner (who died fifty years before Hitler came to power) had founded the Bayreuth Festival as a celebration of German culture, and Hitler was all over it. Each summer, from his rise to power in 1933 to the start of the war in 1939, Hitler had religiously attended the Bayreuth Festival, making the Wagner estate, Wahnfried, his second home. That's why I was so curious to visit it—a place where Hitler had actually stayed.

As we drove into town, it became clear, however, that Bayreuth had taken a terrible pasting from the air. Although a good part of the town had been destroyed, the famous Festspielhaus and a part of Wagner's house were in good repair. The villa itself seemed empty when we entered, but we were soon met by three young servant girls, who turned out to be Polish slave laborers. They wore nondescript workers' uniforms and had telltale numbers tattooed on their forearms. But the girls were nonetheless vivacious and pretty.

The villa was in two parts: a rather modern structure, where we were, and an older and larger one adjacent to it, which had been badly damaged. The Polish girls seemed delighted to see us and showed us into a nicely furnished living room with a grand piano. Les, who had some musical ability, immediately sat down at the piano and began playing dance tunes, which the girls could not get enough of. From then on, to my chagrin, the only one they were interested in was Les. But the girls were only willing to go so far. When it came to sleeping arrangements, we were strictly on our own. They showed us to a bedroom in the newer section of the villa, explaining the room had been built by Frau Wagner, the composer's widow, as a place for her beloved Führer to stay when he was in Bayreuth.

After the girls left, Les and I exchanged a look of disbelief—they expect us to sleep in Hitler's bedroom? It seemed a little creepy—would evil energy still be permeating the space somehow? Ultimately, our exhaustion and the sheer absurdity of the situation trumped everything. Why the hell not?

Moments later, there was a knock on the door and in walked two lieutenant colonels, the battalion commanders of our two sister artillery battalions, Art Peterson and Bill Hasselback.

"What are you fellows doing here?" they asked rather sternly.

But then they smiled, amused at the situation they had just encountered. Like Davis and me, the two battalion commanders clearly had time on their hands and so had left their units to see the sights. I can only imagine what Colonels Peterson and Hasselback must have thought when they discovered the two of us making ourselves comfortable in Hitler's bed.

# 18

# IF THE WAR IS OVER, WHY ARE THEY STILL SHOOTING AT US?

**PATTON'S THIRD U.S. ARMY** was only 200 miles from Berlin, but the Soviets were even closer. On April 30, 1945, Hitler, who was living fifty feet beneath the Chancellery in a concrete bunker, shot himself to death. The Soviets entered Berlin shortly afterward, and the chance for the Third Army to get there was gone. Instead, Patton was ordered to enter Czechoslovakia. But no sooner had we crossed the Czech border than we began to hear rumors of contention between Allied and Soviet headquarters about boundaries. We did not know the details, just that Eisenhower had drawn a line of demarcation fairly close to Czechoslovakia's western border. To Patton's great chagrin, this line was as far east as his forces were allowed to go.

Patton had a right to be upset: there was nothing to stop his Third Army from taking over most of the country, rather than just a narrow strip of land (which might have spared the Czech people forty years of oppression under the Soviets).

What stopped Patton cold was a concession made by FDR and Churchill in Yalta.

By mid-February (while Roosevelt was still alive), it had seemed pretty clear that Britain, Russia, and the U.S. would prevail in the war, and the soon-to-be victorious leaders had convened for a summit meeting on the Black Sea. But the Russians held most of the cards at the Yalta Conference. The Red Army was three times the size of all combined Allied forces in the West, and, at that point, the Russians were only sixty-five miles from Berlin. Roosevelt needed help from the Soviets in the ongoing war against Japan. He also wanted them to be part of the postwar United Nations, which Stalin agreed to on the condition that all permanent members of the Security Council be given veto power over all UN resolutions. Thus, Yalta ended with a provisional agreement between the three Allied powers, albeit fairly lopsided in the Soviets' favor, and this is what forced Patton to tell us two months later to pitch our tents just fifty miles into Czechoslovakia.

My battalion ended up outside of Blatná, a small town of several thousand people thirty-five miles south of Pilsen on a line of demarcation drawn by Eisenhower. Situated in the rolling western Bohemian countryside, it was a paradise of grassy fields, small knolls, lots of ponds, and many lakes to swim in. There were picturesque trails on which we could ride confiscated German army horses. With warm, sunny spring weather, it was a little slice of heaven—particularly after what we'd been through.

After another long period of noncommunication, I wrote home in a state of euphoria:

> We've pretty well cleaned up the area ... and life is wonderful.
> We are in a beautiful lake section and we go swimming all

day long. We're all brown as berries from lying naked in the sunshine, and feel great. Yesterday we went over to a camp of captured German cavalry and relieved them of their horses. I have a beautiful 2 year-old of my own, and plan to take him with me when we go back to Germany. He belonged to a kraut cavalry officer and is a real beauty.

We have movies here nightly, and these make a big hit with the gals. Now, what with swimming, riding and movies, the war seems like a forgotten memory. Thank God it's over— I can't believe it yet!!

One of the reasons it hadn't quite sunk in for me was that we still faced some very precarious situations. There continued to be sporadic, but nonetheless deadly, enemy fire from escaping German SS troops who refused to surrender (undoubtedly knowing what was in store for them if they did). Yet it was all too easy for us to bask in our victory and let down our guard, which is exactly what we did when we set off one afternoon for a picnic.

A group of us loaded up two jeeps with sandwiches and hard-boiled eggs from the mess truck, and went driving off, stopping at the first beautiful lake that caught our fancy. There were six of us on the expedition—myself, plus five enlisted men, including Pete Stakonis, my sergeant at the time. We noticed a large, beautiful rock out in the water that looked perfect for sunbathing. So we swam to it and sat on its smooth surface, sunning ourselves, eyes shut, not a care in the world. After a while, some of us returned to the water to cool off for a bit. But not Sergeant Stakonis—he remained tanning himself on the rock, when suddenly a shot rang out from the woods. Stakonis yelled and started bleeding. He had been hit in the collarbone, which was incredibly lucky. Six inches lower and he'd have been a goner.

The rest of us leaped out of the water and tried to search the area, but the assailant had fled. Someone drove off to get medical help, while others swam back to apply a tourniquet to Stakonis on the rock. I was enraged by the pointlessness of it. What did the triggerman hope to gain from shooting another American? It was like those Volkssturm teenagers in their futile ambush of our column, which unceremoniously ended their all-too-short lives, along with those of some Americans—and for what? This Czech incident was even more absurd. Germany had officially surrendered two days prior. The war was over. Or was it?

When that shot rang out, my psyche kicked back into battle mode with alarming rapidity. It was so unsettling—one moment relaxing, carefree, the next, life and death again. This was my first taste of the uncertainty soon to be my constant, if elusive, companion—lurking below the surface, but ever-present. (God forbid I should allow myself to be complacent.)

No, the war was *not* over. Certainly not for that SS shooter in the woods—scared, unhinged, away from his homeland. And not for me.

From then on, until we left Czechoslovakia, all of us were jumpy about being in our new recreational mode with murderous SS lurking in the area. And it would be years, in fact, before the low-grade rattling inside of me would finally settle into some form of mental armistice.

. . .

I met a marvelous girl while we were in Czechoslovakia. Mila. She was the daughter of the mayor of Kasejovice, near Blatná, where we'd set up camp. Mayor Baranova was one of the many locals who had come to greet us when we arrived and make us feel welcome. After six years of German occupation, the Czechs were overjoyed to see us. (They had no clue—poor souls—that they'd soon be under Stalin's thumb.) It was a brief interlude, but it left a lasting impression in my mind. Here's my letter home:

> The girls in Czechoslovakia are most attractive, with the most beautiful figures I've seen in Europe. They are all brown from the sun, and in their dirndls . . . are truly lovely. By now most of us have acquired steady dates and the name of mine is Mila (nickname in Czech: Milloosha)—a very nice girl who speaks a little English—this comes in very handy as I don't sprechen any Czech. Morally speaking, these girls are strictly well brought up over here, and after the easy conquests of France, Luxembourg, Belgium and the kraut fraus, the men are really griping.

Mila was friendly, lively, and seemed smart. I say "seemed" because we communicated mostly by sign language and smiles—she spoke Czech and German but no French, and only a tiny bit of English. Yet we clicked, and I felt instantly comfortable in her company, as I believe she did in mine.

My acquaintance with Mila and our delightful stay in Czechoslovakia were short-lived, however. With the Soviets pressing to occupy the country and the U.S. and Eisenhower not prepared to stand in their way, we were ordered back to Germany on May 28, 1945, saying good-bye to our newfound friends and pledging to stay in close touch. This pledge was hard to carry out due to the reestablishment of censorship by the Czech Communist regime in 1948, a practice later reinstated by the Soviet regime in 1968 after the brief Prague Spring. But, life often being circular, Mila and I did, in fact, meet again.

In 1992 I went back with two Czech friends from Prague, Professor Oldrich Fejfar and his wife, Tushi, to my old stomping ground in western Bohemia. We were hoping to find the lake where I had been swimming when the SS wounded Pete Stakonis, and, although we knew it a long shot, we decided to also see if Mila Baranova was still around.

The first thing we noticed and were amazed by was the large number of plaques in every village we passed through, thanking the brave Soviet forces, not Patton's Third Army, for the village's liberation. The plaques were apparently installed in 1955 and were backed by textbooks in Czech schools crediting the Soviets for routing the Germans in western Bohemia. When I told villagers that I had been there in 1945, they looked at me in surprise. "But wasn't it the Russians who were here?"

We never did find the lake and its rock, despite looking at a great many lakes. Finally, we drove to Kasejovice to try to find Mila. My Czech friends approached a man in the village square and inquired if he knew of the daughter of the former town mayor. He smiled and lit up: "Of course."

"But Mila doesn't live here anymore," he continued. "She moved to Prague a long time ago."

Though I was disappointed, it seemed pretty obvious to me that someone as bright and vivacious as Mila wouldn't have stayed long in a small town like Kasejovice. But the man was not quite finished. "Today, however, you're in luck."

He explained that Mila just happened to have come from Prague that very day to visit her ninety-two-year-old father. Excitedly, we followed the local to the former mayor's house, knocked on the door, and a rather small, older woman opened it and looked at us, wondering who the devil we were. Oldrich started talking a mile a minute in Czech, and you could see her face freeze in amazement as he said: "This friend of ours, here, is an American who says he knew you during World War II. Do you remember him?" Mila, caught without any forewarning, looked at me—it had been forty-seven years— and, after some hesitation, said: "Roger."

Her father, on learning who I was, stood up and said in English: "It is a great honor, sir." Mila's husband appeared suddenly; though understandably wary at being suddenly faced with three unknown interlopers, including an American, he kindly offered us a drink. As I sipped the liquor, I gazed at Mila in wonder. It was only a week that we had spent together, nearly half a century ago—and yet those days, like precious others in the war, had remained etched with heightened clarity in my mind, and apparently also in Mila's. To those of us who survived that horrendous war, the fleeting moments of joy got earmarked as special treasures in a way that made them stand out from the bleaker memories. That's why I had traveled back to Czechoslovakia at age seventy. It was one of several pilgrimages I'd be compelled to make in order to make peace with what I'd experienced during battle.

. . .

The war did not end the way we had expected it to. I had wanted a sense of finality, I suppose—a feeling of closure. But that's not what happened. Only a handful of generals were present to receive German signatures on the statements of unconditional surrender. To us—the boots on the ground—it was a different experience; we were simply told to stop shooting. But we were not free to go home just yet.

I ended up spending another four months in Europe, as part of the occupying force in Germany, which was both uneventful and odd. All the murderous feelings pent up over the months of combat needed to be suppressed or redirected. We were peacekeepers now and were expected to behave as such. It was not an easy transition, as I wrote home to my dad in late May:

> The last nine months have changed us, and all of us did a little too much killing for our own good. It was the only pleasure we had. We will have to learn to be civilized again and get used to quiet and lack of excitement. I'm afraid I shall always want to kill Germans as long as I live—nothing will ever make me change my mind about them.

My casual expressions about killing must have continued to upset my family; they certainly don't sit well with me now. In any event, my desire to actually *kill* Germans quickly disappeared postwar, although my loathing remained for a considerable period of time.

Not much happened during the occupation, save that Bob Parker met a displaced Frenchwoman named Jacqueline whom he ended up marrying, which underscored my own loneliness and lack of tether. I requested two weeks' leave in England to reconnect with Edna, but the experience left us both a bit unsatisfied. I wasn't myself and would not be so for some time. Edna sensed that I was not quite present— my body was there, my mind elsewhere—but she was a good sport about it. She arranged for a five-day trip to visit Scotland, where I made an impulsive and fairly foolish purchase on the streets of Edinburgh of a not-yet-housebroken mongrel puppy that I loved dearly and called "Mr. Potts." Had I been of sounder mind, I might have foreseen that Mr. Potts would be a large nuisance at this stage of my life, creating problems in London, Riedenburg, on the troopship to New York, and in my parents' carefully maintained apartment in San Francisco. Nevertheless, Mr. Potts became a sort of totem for me, a misguided way to grasp at happiness.

As for Edna, she must have found my behavior rather odd. Unlike some of my friends who got engaged while in England, I had chosen to attach myself to a dog. Frankly, I don't recall exactly what we said to one another during that last visit to England, but I realized later that my behavior had been less than stellar and apologized to Edna in a letter written upon my return to San Francisco:

> The war, to me, became smooth sailing after I met you. The fact that I knew you were on my side . . . meant for a confidence in myself that I think might otherwise have been lacking. And although perhaps I never told you—I was in love with you, too. And that made fighting the Germans easier, instead of harder.
>
> Later on in the war, a blood-thirsty feeling seemed to develop among many of us, myself included, and now that I have shed it, I feel very much ashamed to think that I must have had a very bad taste of it when I came to England on leave last July. . . . I think we had both looked forward to spending some time together for so long, that we almost expected too much. . . . I know, too, that I behaved like a selfish, spoiled, first-class damn fool towards you and everything

else. . . . There were very few people who would have been as fine and as sweet as you were to me in that combative, chip-on-the-shoulder mood I was in.

Upon our return to London, I found a brief moment of solace on Curzon Street, while attending a service at the Christian Science church. Being in the quiet and gentle environment of my church once again, I felt a sense of protection, which was most welcome after so long a period of anxiety and fright. The lesson was on "Truth," something that was beginning to elude me. While I did feel calmer and more at ease as I listened to the Christian Science readers, my ability to process things and make decisions was rapidly eroding. Beneath the surface, and unrecognized by me at the time, I was malfunctioning emotionally and mentally. My ability to think, plan, and act started to desert me and got worse in the days and months to come. I had come through combat physically unscathed and the world should have been my oyster—but as it turned out, it was a world I could no longer enjoy.

# 19

# HOME, NOT SO SWEET

**WHAT A PSYCHIATRIST** would have made of my emotional state in 1945 I can only guess, but I think he would have found it considerably out of balance. I returned home to San Francisco in September, dog in hand, but not exactly a happy camper. My father took pains to make me feel welcome; my mother didn't quite know what to make of me and, not surprisingly, despised Mr. Potts.

There were two people I was hoping to see and be with after the war: Bill Houston, who was from Pulaski, Tennessee, and George Jackson, from Kenilworth, Utah. Both had served overseas, but our friendship predated the war. Given my state of mind, I needed to be with people who knew me well and also knew what I had been through.

Bill and I had worked together in a Northern California lumber camp in 1938. The camp was owned by a mutual family friend, and the two of us were camp "outsiders" (all the other camp workers were professional lumberjacks). Our closest lumberjack friend was killed by the electric saw used to cut the logs, and his death brought Bill and me very close.

George Jackson, whom I had known at Stanford, was extraordinary in every way—one of the most powerful individuals I have ever met. Raised in a tiny Mormon town where his father was the superintendent of a nearby coal mine, George became president of his high school and won a rare state scholarship to attend the school of his choice. He chose Stanford, where he also became student body president, even though he ran against one of the most popular students on campus, an all-American football star, no less.

After serving with valor on naval duty in the Atlantic, George, ready for more action, asked to be reassigned in the fight against Japan. On his way to the Pacific, he made a stop in San Francisco, where my parents invited him over to dinner. (My dad was an even bigger George Jackson fan than I was.)

As I puttered around in the days after my return, I told my folks of my intention to reconnect with Bill and George. My father became very grave and sat me down to tell me some bad news. Both George and Bill were dead. Bill had been killed in action in the Far East; George had been murdered by a U.S. Navy serviceman who had gone berserk aboard a ship in the Pacific.

I looked at my dad in shock. The news was devastating. Just prior to leaving Germany, I had learned of the death of another close friend, with whom I had also hoped to reconnect. I had been doing some desk work, reviewing the Third Army's bulletins, which included its casualty compilations. In going over the killed-in-action list, I was distressed to see the name of an old friend from the desert: Bill Sovacool. We had been very close—though he was one of the officers to leave the battalion in Texas when the division went from "heavy" to "light." I had been really looking forward to renewing my friendship with him once we were back home. But this, too, was not to be. A forward observer like me, Bill Sovacool got killed in Germany in April 1945, less than two weeks before VE Day.

When I read of his death my heart sank; it seemed such a senseless loss to me, for a man to die by enemy gunfire with the war only days from being over. Imagining what the men I knew who were killed might have done with their lives if they had survived made their loss even more difficult to accept: Bill Sovacool would have run his own small business; Dude Dent would have had an admirable career as a professional football player, living happily with his beautiful wife and children. John Kelly, with his great interpersonal skills, could well have been an effective corporate personnel director. Bill Houston, an outdoorsman from the get-go, would have enjoyed a life dealing with natural resources; George Jackson, I felt sure, would have gone on to be president of the United States. Sadly, all five were denied the opportunities that belonged to them.

Was it worth it, I wondered—could Hitler and his Nazis have been thwarted by anything short of war? Despite my realization of war's cost, exemplified by these senseless deaths, it also seemed to me that war was the only way Hitler could have been stopped. But what a price to pay!

. . .

My family never mentioned my decorations, wartime activities, or even World War II again. Their silence on the subject made me feel that the war was really over, something well behind us, no longer to be thought about or talked about. A family friend who came to dinner not long after I had returned, Charles Berolzheimer, brought up my winning a Silver Star in tones of admiration—but I felt as if he were talking about something in my far-distant past.

My sole thoughts about World War II were generated by loneliness for my now geographically dispersed comrades: Tom Cooke, Harley Merrick, Jack Merriam, Bill Walsh, Bill Lothian, Bob Parker, and Alex Graham. To my great relief, they eventually began showing up in San Francisco. Bob Parker got stationed at the Presidio, one and a half miles from my home, and we saw a lot of one another. Meanwhile, Alex Graham had been transferred to serve on the staff of General MacArthur in Tokyo, where he and Frances socialized with any number of Japanese intellectuals and persons of influence. One particular standout was Akira Kurosawa, the great international film director, with whom they struck up a longtime friendship. Through Kurosawa they became friends with a much younger person named Mako Matsukata, the scion of one of the great aristocratic families in Japan, whose grandfather had been the longest-serving prime minister during the reign of Emperor Meiji.

I learned all of this when the Grahams came through San Francisco and visited us on their return to the United States. Mako was with them at the time. A worldly, sophisticated, and intelligent man, he had been a student at Principia College in Illinois when Japan attacked Pearl Harbor. Not repatriated until after the war, Mako did not suffer the wartime experiences of his countrymen. Nonetheless, he viewed life with undisguised cynicism, which is what bonded Mako and me. I also took a liking to Mako because we had something unique in common—although he was Japanese and I was Jewish, we had both been brought up in the Christian Science religion, following its precepts, with one notable exception: "Thou shall not drink." We both imbibed heavily at the time.

While the Grahams and Mako were in town, we all attended a dinner party at the Hillsborough home of an elderly patrician couple. The sedate seniors watched Frances Graham in fascinated surprise as she sat opposite them on their living room couch with her skirt hiked up high. I am convinced that Frances wanted to produce this effect. Without a doubt she was a rebel who constantly struggled against the circumstances of her life: an upper-class heritage, family wealth, and her four-star general father.

Interestingly, those epaulet stars eluded her husband, Alex, who never rose above the rank of colonel, though he certainly deserved to. Army-bred, he loved the service and was a born commander. I heard rumors that he had been offered a brigadier general's post that would have required him to remain in Japan for several years but turned the offer down because of Frances's desire to return to America. His allegiance to the army was trumped only by his allegiance to his wife. An army man to the very last breath, Alex Graham died of a heart attack in his mid-sixties while attending an Army-Navy football game.

. . .

One big question I was facing was: what kind of career did I want to pursue? With the war over, a capable young man was expected to do something with himself. Easier said than done. My confusion began even before I returned to San Francisco. I had written home about some misguided plans I had to enroll in a language program at the Sorbonne in Paris or in Biarritz. "It seems like a damn fine opportunity to learn a language and perhaps music and also to have a good time" is what I said. I had also applied to Shrivenham, a military institution in England, an effort that was farcical. Shrivenham had nothing to offer me, given that I had no intention of staying in the army. What was I thinking?

My planning seemed entirely haphazard, like throwing darts at a board of random options. Had I been of sounder mind, I might have considered law or business school, since the GI bill would have covered all of my expenses—or why not the foreign service if I was so intent on staying overseas? What about a graduate program at Oxford or Cambridge, or even a year of travel to clear my head? Never even crossed my mind. I seemed to have lost the ability to focus on anything, making it impossible to think through the possibilities. Planning ahead and making even tentative decisions was not something I could do in my state of mind right after the war. All I had was a vague sense of not quite being ready to go home and wanting perhaps to stay in Europe.

Many of my friends ended up staying in the service, a safe default given the state of disorientation we were in. As a junior officer, you're not required to make any major decisions on your own, particularly in peacetime—you simply follow orders (a desirable scenario if you're feeling zombielike). Those who chose to stay put in the army included Tom Cooke, Don Guild, Jack Merriam, Bob Parker, and Charlie Gillens. Each of these former 94th comrades-in-arms felt they had made a good career choice by continuing to serve (and thus averting the stress of having to transition into civilian life). From my perspective, their professional lives seemed cocooned in a rigid framework requiring few decisions. I, myself, did not feel cut out for a military career; but that meant making decisions on my own, something I was finding next to impossible to do. Harley Merrick was one of the few 94th officers who left the army when I did, and my impression was that, like me, he was still at sea. This raised an unanswered question in my mind: did you have to stay in the army to feel good about yourself?

Unable to see the available options, I landed by default in my father's car business, which was easy and secure, but did nothing to bolster my self-esteem. Being a car salesman was not exactly what I had in mind for myself. Every day was the same routine, and I found the lack of stimulation depressing.

It dawned on me at some point that I might function better if I spent my time doing something other than selling cars. So, in a rare and impulsive burst of initiative, I got off my duff and simultaneously applied for entrance to Harvard Law School and employment at the Central Intelligence Agency. But as much as I tried to shrug off my indecisive state of mind, it must have been all over me in the interviews.

Both institutions turned me down. The admissions officer at Harvard took one look at my mediocre grades from Stanford and said I was too high a risk. A friend of my mother's named Ducky Harrison was a CIA official and offered to help me join this newly formed organization. So from Harvard I went to Washington and met a slew of CIA executives who told me they liked me and to go home and wait until I received a written offer from them. I was thrilled and returned to San Francisco to await the letter's arrival. But the letter never came. The CIA apparently wanted me as much as Harvard Law School—which is to say, not at all.

There was another institution that turned me down—and this one shocked me—the club my dad belonged to. My dad loved that club and had been a member for many years, but when he joined, Jews were apparently welcome. Now, in 1945, when I applied for my own membership, they apologized and told me they needed to limit the number of Jews. I felt insulted. I had just spent eleven months fighting Nazi anti-Semitism on the battlefields of Europe, and here it bites me in my own backyard. Friends of my father intervened, and the club let me in, helping a bit to raise my fragile spirits. (Fortunately, times change, and today the club's policy exemplifies open-mindedness and fairness.)

It eventually occurred to me to find solace in my church— to go and seek out my old, beloved Christian Science practitioner, Mrs. Jacobs. But here, too, I was dealt a depressing blow: Mrs. Jacobs had died while I was serving overseas. I tried praying with other practitioners, but it simply was not the same.

Seeking the companionship and understanding that was eluding me, I thought about Edna. Maybe I should ask her to come over from England. But I remained unsure that we were right for each other, so I sent her a series of mixed signals in my correspondence. A letter might begin: "It's really disgraceful the way I procrastinate about writing." Then, a few lines later, I'd use an endearing nickname and implore: "Please stay available, Poofti."

We tried to speak by phone from time to time, but that proved equally awkward with me feeling tongue-tied and unable to express myself properly. Then in the late spring of 1946 I received a letter from Edna that contained a bombshell: she was engaged to another man. It felt like another rug being pulled from under me. On June 27, I wrote back, begging her to reconsider, and waited in vain for a response—but none came. I went camping for a few weeks with a friend in the High Sierras, above Lake Tahoe, hoping to clear my mind, but I thought of nothing but Edna.

Then came an unexpected turn of events. In August I received a letter from Edna in which she told me her engagement was off. Elated, I ran off to the cable office and sent her an excited telegram, then dispatched a letter the following day, attempting to explain myself:

> Cabling is without doubt the worst way to propose to the girl you love. But in this case it was the quickest. . . . So, Poofti, will you marry me, like a good girl, and come over here just as fast as red tape will allow?
>
> . . . I know that coming over here to marry a big lug like me would be a tremendous step for you to take. I've thought the thing through very carefully and am convinced that as long as we love each other, nothing could ever stop us.

But the truth of the matter was that I hadn't thought it through at all. In fact, I had serious reservations about making this type of commitment, so—despite Edna's favorable response (she was willing to take the first step and come to America)—I dropped the ball. In retrospect, I am deeply ashamed of how I treated Edna, though at the time in my mental fog, I was unaware of my erratic behavior. Many years after the war, I looked Edna up in England, and we met several times after that. The meetings were friendly, but of course we were no longer close. At one point, when we said good-bye, she handed me a pile of my letters that she had kept for thirty years and was now done with.

Despite my remorse over the way I behaved toward Edna, looking back now I am able to muster up a degree of self-compassion for my own lack of clarity. I was, quite simply, confused and indecisive.

The army had trained me for a year and a half to prepare me for combat. But what about teaching me how to reenter into civilian life? Why is it that the army does relatively little to help its soldiers reintegrate into society? The Department of Veterans Affairs is there as a safety net. But what about more proactive programs? God knows we've done this enough times to know that war messes with the minds of service personnel. It should be built into the cost of war as a line item in every military budget—some kind of training program to teach soldiers how to put down their guns, clear their minds, and return to their families and the civilian workforce. Reentry boot camp—I sure as hell needed one.

Indeed, it would take me many years—and several journeys back to the battlefields of Europe—before I felt truly at peace.

# 20

# RETURN TO THE WAR ZONE

**THIRTEEN YEARS AFTER THE WAR'S END** I met and married the love of my life: Nancy Lee Magid. By that time the disorientation of "battle rattle" was largely gone, thanks to a variety of confidence-building experiences, from leading seminars for Mortimer Adler's Great Books program to moderating and co-producing shows for San Francisco's fledgling public television station. Together fifty-seven years now, my wife and I have been blessed with four kids, six grandkids, and many happy memories. I took over my father's car dealership, engaged in politics, and lived a full life, with ups and downs. Yet I never quite achieved a sense of closure for what had happened to me on those battlefields. Part of it was that I didn't fully understand the nature of that kind of trauma.

Then one day I attended a lunch hosted by the Veterans of the Battle of the Bulge, an organization, to which I belonged, of old-timers who'd served in Bastogne in December 1944.

Two psychiatrists spoke about a subject unfamiliar to me: post-traumatic stress disorder. They answered questions and spent the afternoon interviewing us. I met with them several times after that, and we concluded that I had indeed suffered for years from PTSD, an all-too-common occurrence among war veterans. We tried to figure out the moment that my emotional system began to flip: Was it when I shot the two Germans in Normandy? Or shot two more Germans in Heimboldshausen? Or experienced the mayhem at Arracourt? Or shrank from the Nebelwerfer shells that dropped Jack Merriam? It was probably all those events, and then some, that triggered the mental changes that had confounded me for so long.

Learning that I had been suffering from PTSD came as a relief, an answer to a question that had bothered me for a great part of my life. And with the relief came the deepest regret that I had not sought psychiatric help back in 1946, when this realization and processing could have changed my life for the better a good deal sooner. There were a number of respectable psychiatrists in San Francisco in 1946, and all I had needed to do was knock on the door of one of them. But finding the right door meant overcoming the stress and indecision that enveloped me. The stress won out, and I never knocked.

. . .

In 1992 Nancy and I flew to Venice to attend the wedding of a close family friend. After the festivities I decided to take a side trip on my own. We were less than 200 miles from the Czech Republic, so I figured this was a great chance to visit Prague, which I was curious to see, now that the Czechs were once again free of Soviet domination. This was when I had the reunion with Mila and looked for the lake where Sergeant Pete Stakonis had been shot. But the trip didn't begin there. Being so close to Germany, I decided to face those battlefields, too. In particular, I wanted to go back to the concentration camp we had liberated.

I hired a car and driver, who chauffeured me to the town of Ohrdruf. The town was in what had formerly been East Germany, now reunited with its western part. As we motored into the town square, I could feel my pulse quickening. I knew this would not be easy.

The Ohrdruf camp was now a German army base, and I had a letter of introduction to its commanding officer. As we drove through the gates, the place appeared totally different to me: the concentration camp barracks and large yard were no longer there. Captain Riese, a charming and intelligent German army professional who commanded the base, told me that Ohrdruf had been a German army facility since 1908. It became an annex to the Buchenwald concentration camp for only a short time, from 1944 to 1945, but a lot of people died there. The Soviets used it as a base for their forces in East Germany and had 20,000 troops stationed there. It reverted to the Germans in the early 1990s.

Captain Riese and the other officers under his command were forthcoming and unhesitant in their responses to my myriad questions—I felt encouraged about the huge change in character between these Germans and the ones who had been there during World War II.

But, as I stood on the grounds and looked around, I detected a solemn feeling arising within me. Though the place had changed considerably, I sensed something in the ether:

a palpable feeling of the horrific events that had happened here. I was deeply cognizant of the tragic loss of lives—the thousands of Jews and others slaughtered within these walls. Maybe it was just me; I doubt the young German officers serving there had a sense of the gravitas that permeated the soil under their feet. But I sure did. Bob Parker and I had been the first American soldiers to stumble upon a grim scene of devastating carnage that was impossible to erase. Even though nearly fifty years had passed, it was once again vivid in my mind's eye.

Before I left, Captain Riese and another officer took me to the cemetery where the concentration camp victims had been buried. There is a beautiful memorial stone there with words:

Here lie 5,000 prisoners of war from different nations who died in the years 1944 to 1945 in the former outer division of Buchenwald concentration camp. (Camp SIII). City of Ohrdruf.

I found myself welling with emotion—a deep sadness, not just about the loss of lives, but also a somber recognition of the atrocities we humans are capable of. I realized that I, myself, continued to carry deep remorse about certain things that I had done during the war, which is what compelled me to the next stop on my journey.

Some years before this trip, I had lunched with David Fischer, a former career officer in the U.S. Foreign Service who had been consul general in Munich during the 1970s. Unaware of my wartime background, he told me of an official picnic lunch the German municipal government had given him in a forest east of Munich. After lunch, his German host asked him to walk to a nearby glade. Fischer said that when he arrived at the glade he saw that it contained a small cemetery with about twenty to twenty-five headstones. What struck him were two extraordinary circumstances: every headstone had the same date of death—a day in April 1945—and all of those buried there had been sixteen or seventeen years of age. I stared at him and practically gasped: "David, you won't believe what I'm about to tell you." Based on the geography and the date, I knew at once that these must have been the Volkssturm teenagers that we shot after they had attempted to ambush us. I decided then and there that I would one day find that gravesite. And that's exactly what I attempted to do in 1992.

It wasn't easy. David's description of the location had been somewhat vague, not to mention the fact that the landscape had changed dramatically since I'd been there in 1945. My driver and I ended up conducting a ten-hour search of a forty-mile forest corridor running south to north between the towns of Cham and Weiden, the area where I had calculated the incident to have occurred. As we searched, I questioned people at churches, villages, and farms about the whereabouts of Fischer's glade and war graves in general. Older Germans didn't want to talk about the war at all; it was obvious that this was a taboo subject for them. Church personnel were friendly but explained that the government or individual families had long ago removed the graves from the forest. Finally, by mid-afternoon, we met an older gentleman on a farm who knew where some gravesites were and kindly offered to take us to them. All the men buried at this site had been killed in April 1945, but most had died in their forties, though several had been very young. Lacking more specific instructions, this was as close as we were able to get to finding David Fischer's glade.

I was disappointed, and a sense of war-weariness came over me as I stared at the graves of the few German youngsters who had died there. That's when I felt something I had not felt since the war: emotional unease, almost fright. It was a flashback so common among those of us who suffer from PTSD, where it suddenly feels as if the combat stakes are back. I could hear the echoes of imaginary gunfire in my mind and pictured myself back on the autobahn with my unit. It happens once in a great while, even to this day—I'll hear a loud sound in the air that sounds like an artillery shell and, all of a sudden, the whole picture changes. Memories of the war continue to haunt me. And that was particularly apparent in 1992, as I faced those graves, which had propelled me a half-century into my past.

Guilt, again . . . still with me. I felt like apologizing. That's why I had tried so hard to seek out those graves—to stand in contrition before those poor departed souls. Not having found them, I missed a sense of closure—it continued to elude me—and I realized this would not be my last trip back to graveyards in Europe.

. . .

Nancy's brother, Jim Magid, was an avid World War II buff, though he was younger than me and didn't actually serve during the war. Nonetheless, he bought and read every book he could find about the subject, and I found him to be something of an expert on the war. I went back to Europe in 1999 with Jim and two of his sons-in-law, Ian Jones and Michael Diefenbach, to tour some of the battlefields of France and Luxembourg. We had maps and various guidebooks, including the *History of the 94th Artillery Battalion*, which had been compiled right after the war. We walked the windswept sands of Utah Beach, where it all began. We visited Rennes, where we first faced the wrath of the German 88mm guns. We went back to Arracourt where Generals Wood and Patton asked me for directions. We revisited Commercy, where Neil Wallace's 66th Battalion had been decimated by the Luftwaffe and I was forced to inspect the dog tags of the dead. We toured the towns of the Saar Valley, where John Kelly became reckless and lost his life. We went back to Bastogne, where I earned my Silver Star for standing my ground and returning fire in the face of bombardment by the German Luftwaffe.

At Caudan I was surprised (and disappointed) to see no sign of the church steeple, where I had undertaken my first forward observation stint in combat. We thought at first that we had the wrong town. Then, while Jim parked the Mercedes we had rented, I walked over to an older couple standing at an ATM and addressed them in my pigeon French: *Où est l'église?* (Where is the church?)

No church, they responded. The nearest one is miles away. I explained to them that I'd been a soldier here in 1945, and suddenly they went crazy—all animated and gesticulating— knowing exactly what I was talking about. They took me by both arms and frog-marched me up the street to a nice-look-ing building, which was either the town or regional govern-ment headquarters. Escorting me up the stairs to the sec-ond-floor legislative chamber, they pointed excitedly to an old photograph hanging above the house speaker's empty chair. It was the church.

By the time we left the council chambers, they were talking a mile a minute, and we soon found ourselves mobbed by a group of townsfolk, who threw rapid-fire questions at us, most of which I couldn't understand. They were extraordinarily excited to be dredging up this part of the town's history. Eventually, we did manage to communicate and I found out something fascinating—just days after I had used the tower as my OP (and nearly died in it), a German dynamite squad rolled into Caudan, which we had abandoned. Apparently, from my vantage point in the steeple, I had inflicted considerable damage with my firing coordinates. The Germans, angry about their losses and determined not to have such a thing happen again, blew the church and its steeple to smithereens. The town had been churchless ever since.

. . .

Another stop we made on that trip was Troyes, where Dude Dent had his premonition and came to me in desperation, but I was unable to prevent his death. This one was hard for me. I needed to make peace with what happened there.

U.S. servicemen and women who die overseas during wartime are often buried on site in makeshift graves or at local cemeteries, so I thought there was a good chance that Dent had been buried nearby. Determined to find his gravesite, I did what I had done seven years prior in Germany—scoured the area, talked to locals, and visited every cemetery I could find. But I came up dry again and was deeply disappointed.

One place where we managed to see a lot of graves was the American Cemetery in Luxembourg City—where almost all of the headstones, which run as far as the eye can see, belong to soldiers who died during the Battle of the Bulge. There was a graves registry that listed the casualties by unit, and I saw some names from the 94th—no Dude Dent, but I did find another friend: Draper Charles, my former driver, whom I'd defended in the court-martial in the Mojave Desert. Standing before his headstone made the countless others less anonymous, somehow—all of those soldiers had families and friends and people who cared about them. And there was one soldier whom everybody knew: George S. Patton, who died in Germany on December 21, 1945, six months into the occupation.

. . .

I returned to San Francisco not quite satisfied about the excursion, feeling particular disappointment over not having found the grave of Dude Dent. I decided to do some research back home, calling the Army Graves Registration Service, which had been renamed Mortuary Affairs, operating under the Quartermaster Corps. I found out that, according to a 1946 report by the Graves Registration, there were a total of 359 American military cemeteries overseas, containing the remains of 241,500 World War II dead. However, at the time, the estimated total number of U.S. casualties in World War II was listed as 286,959—a discrepancy of over 45,000. And, while a good number of those were the "unknown solders" whom we honor on Memorial Day, many others had been repatriated to cemeteries in America. It turns out that Dude Dent was among those whose remains had been returned home.

Excitedly, I inquired as to where I could find him, expecting to be told Arlington National Cemetery or one of the other military burial grounds near our nation's capital. But, as it turned out, Dude Dent had been buried just fifteen miles from my house at the Golden Gate National Cemetery.

As soon as I learned of this extraordinary coincidence, I drove out to visit Dent's gravesite and pay my respects. Although I was given the grave's location, I had trouble finding it; the face of the gravestone had faded away over the years, and no attempt had been made to restore it. The gravesite appeared unvisited and abandoned. Standing there, looking at the worn gravestone, I felt the full force of the realization that, through the luck of the draw, Dude Dent never got beyond August 23, 1944. I had gone on to have a wife, children, and a long life. Dude got nothing. Seeing his headstone there drove home the capriciousness, perniciousness, and awfulness of war. And I couldn't get over the fact that, of all the places that Dent could have been buried, he ended up in my own backyard.

# EPILOGUE

**"WE'RE STUDYING WORLD WAR II, GRANDPA,"** said my oldest grandson, Kai, one Saturday afternoon not too long ago. "We need guest speakers, and I'm hoping you might want to come."

Happy to participate, I went to his school in the Berkeley hills to address the eighth-grade class. They put on a lunch for the people who participated, which included teachers, students, like my grandson, and actual veterans, though there weren't too many of us still alive. There were widows, too, and one man, Ernest Ostreicher, who was a concentration camp survivor. Each of us addressed the students, then we all stayed for the buffet lunch. Most people stood around, mingling with each other on their feet while eating their meal. But I was tired, so I found a spot to sit. And the man who'd been a concentration camp prisoner, by chance, sat next to me at the same table. He didn't know me, nor did I know him—but, naturally curious, I asked him: "What camp were you in?"

"Orhdruf," he responded.

I couldn't believe my ears. It wasn't possible. I explained to him that Bob Parker and I were the first Americans to open the gates of Orhdruf. Now it was his turn to be astonished. He became very emotional and flung his arms around me, saying: "You're my savior!"

But I was confused. I told him that when Parker and I found the place, nearly all the prisoners had been killed. Ostreicher explained that he had originally been sent to Buchenwald at age seventeen, as a Romanian Jew. In the last years of the war, he was transferred to Orhdruf, a subsidiary of Buchenwald. As the Allies approached the camp in the spring of 1945, the German guards assembled all the able-bodied prisoners and marched them forty-some miles back to Buchenwald. He was nineteen at the time. The forced march, which took place on April 2, was grueling; many died on the way, or fell by the wayside and were shot when they couldn't keep up. Two days later, on April 4, Parker and I arrived at Orhdruf and discovered the pile of corpses—those too weak to move, who'd been executed on the spot. Buchenwald was liberated several days later by other soldiers in Patton's army, and the general himself arrived on April 15.

Thus, I explained to Ostreicher that I was not, in fact, his savior, but he would have nothing of it. He just kept hugging and hugging me—it must have been five minutes—repeating: "You're my savior, you're my savior."

The literal truth of who had walked through the gates of his camp didn't matter to him. The moment had a much deeper meaning for him. What were the odds that his daughter just happened to be a teacher at my grandson's school? It felt like we had been delivered to one another, just like Dude Dent had been buried a stone's throw from my house in San Francisco. Here we were, a soldier and a survivor, locked in an embrace for what seemed like an eternity. It made me feel, finally, that for all the loss and suffering—for the lost lives of Draper Charles, John Kelly, Dude Dent, and countless others—it was worth it. Many more lives were saved through their sacrifice, including that of Ernest Ostreicher.

I'd say, in the final analysis, that he was *my* savior.

With Mila Baranova, in Kasejovice, Czechoslovakia, 1945. We had a good time together, even if we didn't speak the same language.

The officers of the 94th on occupation duty in Germany after the war, in 1945. In the back row, Harry Truitt is on the left end, then Darrell Wood, Sherm McGrew, and me, with Tom Cooke and Jack Merriam on the far right. In the third row, Jacob "Doc" Horowitz is on the far left, and Chief Warrant Officer Reid Bush, a good friend, is fourth from the right. In the second row, Bill Lothian is the third from left, Bob Parker fifth, and Charlie Gillens sixth, with Bill Walsh on the far right end. In front, Don Guild is second from right.

Sitting in our officers' club in Germany after the war, in 1945, are the "Sly-Feelers": (from left) me, Captains Bill Walsh, Harley Merrick, and Tom Cooke. We would never forget our weekend bonding together in liberated Paris after the intense fighting in the Ardennes.

Our battalion surgeon Doc Horowitz in Germany in 1945. A strong personality, respected by everyone, he intervened to keep me with my battalion when I got bronchitis in Luxembourg.

Edna with my newfound puppy, Mr. Potts, in 1945. I was so shaken by the war, suffering from "battle rattle," I couldn't commit myself to anyone or anything, except for this puppy.

More than fifty years after the war's end, in 1999, I returned to some of the battlefields with my brother-in-law Jim Magid and his sons-in-law. One place we checked out was Bastogne, where I'd earned a Silver Star for unhesitatingly shooting back as the German planes attacked and then, under gunfire, rescuing a group of badly injured men.

On Armistice Day, November 11, 2011, I felt gratified to be awarded the Legion of Honor for helping to liberate France from the Nazis during World War II. The French Consul General Romain Serman pinned the medal on me in San Francisco.

This memoir began as a way of telling my family about the ordeal of war. Throughout, I have been supported by my wife of fifty-seven years, Nancy (seated next to me), my four children and their spouses, and my six grandchildren.

# ACKNOWLEDGMENTS

**PULLING TOGETHER A MEMOIR** of events from seventy years ago was quite an undertaking. I had great editorial help over the years. At the end, my developmental editor, Peter Rader, was simply outstanding in helping to make the war come alive—in all its horror, devastation, and occasional humor. Fiona Maazel and Liza Birnbaum were most helpful in the early days of the writing. Deborah Kirshman, my editorial adviser, and Sue Heinemann, my copy editor, were instrumental in the final editing.

Three of my Fourth Armored comrades helped me retrace our combat days. Lieutenant Colonel Bob Parker, my old battalion commander, remembered every single detail of our eleven months of fighting. Tom Cooke remembered all the political in-fighting in the battalion. And Wayne Seaman, a fellow forward observer, remembered in detail the battle of Troyes. Corporal Albert Maranda kept a combat diary, which is in print and which I found invaluable.

Photographs came forward from my old World War II English friend Joan Hills of herself and Edna. Peter Boswell, Edna's son, provided more photos of his mother. Tom Cooke's son, Steve, also contributed photographs, as did Bob Parker's son, John.

My family—including my children, John, Christopher, Anthony, and Lucy—was always supportive as I worked on this memoir over the years. My brother-in-law, Jim Magid, accompanied me back to Europe on many a trip, helping me to locate former battle sites with his understanding of how the topography might have changed after so many years. Often Jim's sons-in-law, Ian Jones and Michael Diefenbach, traveled with us, with Ian assisting in pinpointing the battle sites and Michael, born in Germany after the war, adding a valuable perspective as well as translation skills. In addition, my friends Oldrich and Tushi Fejfar kindly aided me with my exploration of old haunts in Czechoslovakia.

But over the many years I worked on the memoir, no support was more extraordinary than the help I got from my dear, beloved wife, Nancy. Nancy was there with me every step of the way, as she has been throughout our almost sixty years of married life. Her unfailing support was instrumental in getting this manuscript written.

# INDEX

*Page numbers in italics refer to photographs*

## A

Abrams, Lieutenant Colonel
Creighton (Abe), 56–57, 127, 144; at
Arracourt, 147, 148; at Assenois, 163
Adler, Mortimer: Great Books
program, 222
*Admiral Graf Spee,* 9
African Americans, in army, 31–33,
94–95
*Afrika Korps,* 43, 66
Airburst shells, 151
Allen, Colonel Henry B., 12, 20,
21, 23
America First Committee, 10–11
Andrews, Lois, 51
Anti-Semitism, 3–4; in Nazi
Germany, 7–8, 9, 95, 190, 198

(*see also* Concentration camps); in
Palm Springs, 49; of Patton, 121;
postwar, 219; at Stanford, 11; of
Wagner, 199
Ardennes Offensive, 161–67
Arlon (Belgium), 123, 161, 162
Army Graves Registration Service,
230
Arracourt (France), 147–51, 154, 156,
163, 228
Assenois (Belgium), 162–63
Asthma, 12, 19–22
Athienville (France), 149, 151
Atlantic Wall, 86–87
Auschwitz concentration camp, 172
Avranches (France), 119, 121, 123, 139

**B**

Bailey, Lieutenant Colonel Ed, 44
Baranova, Mayor, 206, 208, 224
Baranova, Mila, 206–8, *235*
Barneville (France), 112
Bastogne (Belgium), 123, 139, 161,
    163–67, 222, 228, *237*
Bathlemont (France), 151
Battalion liaison officer's job, 183–84
Battery officers, 38–39, 43, 74
Battle of Britain, 10, 90
Battle of the Bulge, 161–67; gravesite,
    229–30; Veterans of, 222
Battle rattle. *See* Post-traumatic
    stress disorder
Bayreuth (Germany), 196, 199–201
Berlin (Germany), 202, 203
Berolzheimer, Charles, 215
Bezange-la-Petite (France), 151
Bixby, Colonel Ernest, 91, 132, 143
Blair, Charlie, 170
Blatná (Czechoslovakia), 203–5
Blue, Ben, 62
Boas, Benjamin (father), 2, 4–5,
    12, 25, 26, 40, 69, 78, 177; at
    Camp Ibis/Las Vegas, 64–65;
    and Downey, 153; European trip
    (1935) and, 82; flask from, 80;
    in Palm Springs, 49–50; Pontiac
    dealership, 15, 49, 92, 222;
    postwar relationship with son,
    212, 213; support for son's joining
    field artillery, 18; *see also* Letters
    home
Boas, Kai (grandson), 232
Boas, Larie (mother), 2, 5, 25, 26,
    40, 69, 80, 100, 196; on European

trip (1935), 6, 8–9, 82, 169; in
    Palm Springs, 49–50; postwar
    relationship with son, 212;
    proposed Texas visit, 77–78; vs.
    son's joining field artillery, 16–18,
    39; *see also* Letters home
Boas, Nancy Lee Magid (wife), 222,
    223, *238*
Bourke-White, Margaret, 192
Bradley, General Omar N., 160, 191,
    192
Brandt, Billie, 65–66, *108*
Bristol (England), 90
British army, 10, 13, 34–35, 89; in
    Africa, 66; Martin hoax of, 85–86
Bronze Star, 132
Buchenwald concentration camp,
    190, 192–93, 224, 233
Burkett, Nancy, 15
Burton, Nadine, 124
Bush, Chief Warrant Officer Reid, *235*

**C**

Camp Bowie (Texas), 67, 73–79
Camp Ibis (Mojave Desert), 63–66,
    *103*
Camp Ord (California), 27
Camp Roberts (California), 24–30, 31
Capital punishment, 2–3
Caudan (France), 123, 127–32, 139,
    191; return to, 228–29
Cecil, Captain, 35, *71*
Charles, Private Draper, 60, 163,
    229–30, 234
Chemnitz (Germany), 199
Christian Science, 1–2, 18, 20, 216;
    as postwar solace, 211, 219

Churchill, Sir Winston, 203
Click, Lieutenant Ralph M. (Morris), 75–76, 113
Cline, Lieutenant Ken, 72
Clochimont (Luxembourg), 168
Codman, Colonel Charles R., 192
Coffman, Owen, 49
Commercy (France), 139–44, 147, 165; post-battle, 145–47, 228
Communications classes, 36
Concentration camps, 172, 180, 189–93, 198–99, 224–25, 232–34
Connolly, Lieutenant Colonel R. M., 132, 133
Cooke, Lieutenant/Captain Tom, 52, 53, 54, 57, 65, 77, 100, 177, 235, 236; Abrams and, 148; Joan Hills and, 93–94, 101; in Paris, 169, 171; postwar, 215, 217–18; promotion, 79, 183; in Vannes, 127
Coutances (France), 117–18, 121
Creel, George, 5
Crosby, Bing, 145
Czechoslovakia, 195, 202–7; return visit to, 207–8, 223–4; SS shooter in, 204–5

**D**

Daniels, Bebe, 97
Davis, Lieutenant Les, 199–201
D-Day (Operation Neptune), 87, 97–98, 109, 112–13
Dent, Lieutenant Lewis (Dude), 113–14, 133, 135–37, 139, 214, 234; grave of, 229–31, 233
Department of Veterans Affairs, 221
*Der Stürmer* weekly, 7

Devers, General Jacob, 50, 60
Devizes (England), 88–89; Wrens and, 93–94
Diefenbach, Michael, 227
Downey, Senator Sheridan, 153–54
DuBovy, Alex, 142, 143

**E**

Eddy, Major General Manton, 160
Eddy, Mary Baker, 1, 2
88mm German guns, 125–26
Eisenach (Germany), 187
Eisenhower, General Dwight D., 66, 83; at concentration camp, 191–92; demarcation line of, 202, 203, 206; Eddy and, 160; letter to Allied Expeditionary Force, 99
Emmett, Private Paul, 183
Enemy, demonization of, 6, 117, 119–20; *see also* Propaganda
England: arrival in, 84–85; postwar visit to, 209–10; wartime life, 87–90; wishes for leave to, 176–77
Enlisted men, 28, 54, 75
European trips: in 1935, 6, 8–9, 169, 170, 179; in 1992, 207–8, 223–26; in 1999, 227–30

**F**

Faringdon (England), 93, 94
Fear: belligerence and, 180, 188; combat and, xi, 84, 109, 114, 128, 156, 166; letter writing and, 152; prayer and, 149–50; "Section Eight" discharge and, 111; *see also* Post-traumatic stress disorder
Fejfar, Oldrich and Tushi, 207, 208

51st Armored Infantry Battalion, 181

53rd Armored Infantry Battalion, 163

Fischer, David, 225–26

Fischer, Louis, 8

Fitzgerald, Barry, 145

Flinchum, Sergeant James, 75

Fort Bragg (North Carolina), 41–43, 72

Fort Sill (Oklahoma), 27, 29–30, 41, 70–71; training, 31–40, 42–43, 46

Forward observers, xiii, 38–39, 43, 46–47, 74, 113–15, 133, 184; in airplanes, 157, 189; at Caudan, 128–32; at Commercy, 140–42; at Troyes, 135–37

Fourth Armored Division, 67, 73, 79, 143; move to France, 99, 101–2, 109–11, 113; in Normandy, 109–21, 139; Patton and, 37, 119, 159, 174; shipment to England, 80–81, 83–84; *see also* 94th Armored Field Artillery Battalion *and specific officers*

Fourth Infantry Division, 112–13

Franco, Francisco, 85

French Forces of the Interior (FFI), 124; and Rennes, 125–26

Friendly fire incidents, 119, 139, 173

**G**

Gay, Lieutenant General Hobart R., 192

George VI, King: D-Day announcement of, 97–98

German American Bund, 11

Germany: fighting in, 181–201;

occupying force in, 206, 209–10; surrender of, 208–9

Geronimo, 31

Gershwin, George, 110

Gillens, Lieutenant/ Major Charlie, 52, 54, 55, 77, 104, 107 235; daughter's birth, 153; postwar, 217–18

Gillens, Mary, 77

Glew, Edna Frances, 92–94, 97, 98, 108, 236; in letters to parents, 100–101, 177; postwar relationship with, 209–11, 219–21

Goebbels, Joseph, 6

Goldberg, Rachel (great-grandmother), 1, 2

Goldsmith, Captain Roger, 12–13

Gotha (Germany): ambush on road to, xii, 188–89

Graham, Lieutenant Colonel/ Colonel Alex, 50, 79, 100, 107; audit requested by, 58; at Caudan, 130–31, 132, 133, 141, 143–44; at Commercy, 142; in Coutances, 117–18; leadership skills of, 50, 56–57, 112, 146; letter-writing requested by, 154; on Paris, 171; postwar, 215, 216; socializing with, 60–61, 76, 215, 216; translation request of, 124; at Wood's wedding, 89

Graham, Dr. Bill, 61

Graham, Frances, 50–51, 56, 60–61, 76–77; postwar, 215, 216; pralines for, 78–79

Graves registration, 142–43

Green, Dr. Aaron, 21

Grush, Lieutenant Ken, 72

Guébling (France), 160, 163

Guild, Lieutenant Don, 89, *104*, 139, 186, *235;* postwar, 217–18

Gunnery classes, 28, 35, 37–39, 46–47

**H**

Hanau (Germany), 185, 186, 187

Harrison, Ducky, 218

Hasselback, Lieutenant Colonel Bill, 200–201

Heimboldshausen (Germany), 182, 187

Helmes (Germany), 187

Hemingway, Ernest, 112

Hills, Joan, 93–94, 101

Hitler, Adolf, 5, 6, 14, 45, 214; anti-Semitism of, 2, 7, 11, 95; early victories of, 13; Martin hoax and, 86; mistakes of, 16; Rommel and, 66–67, 86; Stalin and, 8, 13; suicide, xii, 147, 202; Wagner's villa and, 199–201

Hoffman, Lieutenant Albert, 136

Holocaust, 180; *see also* Concentration camps

Horowitz, Captain Jacob (Doc), 62, 92–93, 136, *235, 236;* at Bastogne, 166; on Boas's bronchitis, 172, 176; at Üdersdorf, 183

Houston, Bill, 212–13, 214

Howitzers: horse-drawn 75mm, 12, 29; mobile 105mm, 29, 30, 38, *105, 106,* 126

Hull, Cordell, 20

**I**

IG Farben, 190–91

**J**

Jackson, George, 212, 213, 214

Jacobs, Maude V., 18, 20, 21, 22, 23, 219

Jessel, George, 51

Johnston, Warden James, 3

Jones, Ian, 227

Juvelize (France), 156

**K**

Kasejovice (Czechoslovakia), 206–8

Keefe, Lieutenant, 32

Kelly, Lieutenant John, 52, 53–54, *107,* 113–14, 153, 214; death of, 155–56, 181, 228, 234

Killing, act of, 42, 116–17, 178–79, 180, 188

Klein (later Kline), Annie (grandmother), 2, 26, *69,* 78, 82, 169; letters to, 67–68, 100, 179, 181–82

Klein, Sigmund, 82

Kurosawa, Akira, 215

**L**

Lane, Sergeant Richard J., 186

Languimberg (France), 160

Las Vegas (Nevada), 63–65

Leach, Captain Jimmie, 148

Legion of Honor award, *237*

Letters home: belligerence in, 178–80, 184, 188, 194, 209; from Czechoslovakia, 203–4, 206; from England, 87–88, 92, 100–101,

(Letters home, cont.) 102–103; from
France, 127, 145–46, 154, 160, 171;
gap in, 152–54; from Germany,
184–85, 209; from Luxembourg,
176–77; from Paris, 171; on postwar
future, 181–82, 209; from U.S.
camps, 25, 28, 32–33, 34, 37, 58,
67–68, 74, 75, 76, 80
Lezey (France), 151
*Life* magazine, 192
London (England), 91–92; D-Day
announcement in, 97–98;
postwar visit to, 211
Lorient (France), 123, 127; *see also*
Caudan
Lothian, Lieutenant/Captain Bill,
52, 53, 74, *107*, 113, 215, 235;
at Commercy, 141–42, 187; at
Heimboldshausen, 187; Silver
Star, 187–88; in Vannes, 127
Louisiana, 78
*Lusitania*, 5
Luxembourg, 168–69, 172–77, 178;
return to, 227, 229–30
Lyon, Ben, 97

**M**

MacArthur, General Douglas, 215
Magid, James (Jim; brother-in-law),
227, 228
Maginot Line, 10
Main River, 185–86
Martin, Major William, hoax, 85–86
Matsukata, Mako, 215–16
Matzger, Dr. Edward, 21
McGrew, Lieutenant Sherman
(Sherm), 139, 186, 188, 235

McNair, Lieutenant General Lesley
J., 119, 139, 173
Memorial Day, 230
Mericle, Dr. Earl (Doc), 111
Merriam, Lieutenant/Captain Jack,
182–83, 223, 235; postwar, 215,
217–18
Merrick, Lieutenant/Captain Harley,
*108*, 157–58, 169, 178, 186, *236*;
postwar, 215, 218
Messerschmitt (ME) 109s, 141, 142,
166, 186
Metz (France), 139, 147
Mojave Desert Training Center,
44–68, *103–7*; simulations at, 58;
*see also* Camp Ibis
Moldovan, Belle, 179–80
Montgomery, General Bernard,
34–35, 86
Moselle River, 140, 147, 154
Motors classes, 28–29, 36, 37
Mussolini, Benito, 86

**N**

Nancy (France), 139, 147; leave in,
157–58
*Nebelwerfers* (screaming meemies),
119, 183
94th Armored Field Artillery
Battalion, 45, 79, 227, *235*;
batteries of, 74; in Belgium, 139,
161–67; in Brittany, 123–33, 139;
in Champagne region, 134–38,
139; in Czechoslovakia, 203–5,
206; in England, 84–102; first
day of battle, 114–17, 139; forward
observers in, 113–15, 136; in

Germany, 181–201, 206, 209–10; in Lorraine, 139–51, 154–60; in Luxembourg, 168–69, 172, 176, 178; in Normandy, 109–21, 124, 139; route map for, *vi–vii;* social life of in Mojave Desert, 50–51, 52–53, 60–61; *see also* Fourth Armored Division *and specific officers and battles*

Normandy (France): Allied invasion, 98, 109–21, 124, 154

Nystrom, First Lieutenant Bertil, 114, 139

**O**

Obersgegen (Germany), 181

O'Connor, Francis, 183

Ohrdruf concentration camp, xiii–xiv, 189–92; Ostreicher at, 232–34; return visit to, 224–25

Operation Neptune. *See* D-Day

Orléans (France), 132, 134

Orsbon, Sergeant Herman, 139

Ostreicher, Ernest, 232–34

**P**

Palm Springs (California), 49–50, 58

Paris (France): Nazi occupation, 110, 171–72; weekend visit to, 169–72

Parker, Captain/Lieutenant Colonel Robert (Bob), 55, 56, 74, 76, 100, 107, 144, 169, 235; at Arracourt, 148; at Bastogne, 167; Boas's father and, 65; at Caudan, 128; Dent's premonition and, 136, 137; on forward observers, 114; on Kelly, 155; Lothian's Silver

Star and, 187; at Main River, 186; marriage of, 209; at Ohrdruf, xiii, 189–91, 225, 232, 233; postwar, 215, 217–18; promotion, 146; at Üdersdorf, 183

Patton, General George S., 66, 86, 87, 98, 119; at Arracourt, 150, 228; at Avranches, 121–22, 139, 150; Commercy wait and, 145, 147; at concentration camps, 191–93, 233; in Czechoslovakia, 202–3; Desert Training Center and, 44; gravesite, 230; hospital visit in Luxembourg City, 22–23, 173–76; Lorient attack and, 127; at Prince Maurice Barracks, 95–97, 150; in Sicily, 96; at Singling, 158–59, 160

Pearl Harbor attack, 15

Peterson, Lieutenant Colonel Art, 200–201

Plas, Sergeant Bob, 115–16, 118, 179; at Caudan, 128, 129, 130, 131

Poland: Hitler's attack on, 13; 1935 visit, 8

Porter, Cole, *Panama Hattie,* 97

Post-traumatic stress disorder (PTSD, or battle rattle), xiv, 42, 96, 154, 166–67, 182, 205, 221–22; flashback and, 227; postwar indecisiveness as, 182, 211, 217–21

Potts, Mr. (dog), 210, 212, 236

Powell, Lieutenant George, 22, 114, 139

Powers, Major Lloyd, 58–59, 60, 64, 144, 146

Prague Spring, 207

Prince Maurice Barracks (England), 88; Patton at, 95–97

Propaganda, 5–6; in Nazi
Germany, 7

**R**

Ramsenthal (Germany), 199
Rennes (France), 123, 125–26, 134,
228
Rhine crossing, 185
Riese, Captain, 224, 225
Rimsdorf (France), 160
Roach, Spider, 4
Romania, 9
Rommel, General/Field Marshal
Erwin, 43, 66, 86–87, 97
Roosevelt, President Franklin
Delano, 10, 20; death of, 195–96;
proclamation of war, 16; at Yalta,
203
Rorem, Private Eiden, 183
ROTC training, 11–14, 17
Rumelange (Luxembourg), 168–69,
176
Russian troops, 164, 195, 199,
202, 203; Czech plaques
honoring, 207

**S**

Saar Valley, 157–60, 161, 228
Sainteny (France): 94th's first day of
battle, 114–17, 139
Salinger, J. D., 112
Salisbury Plain (England): firing
practice, 90–91
*Santa Paula*, 83, 84
Schlitz (Germany), 187
Schwabhausen (Germany), 195
Seaman, Lieutenant Wayne, 136

Segregation, in army, 32, 94
Sens (France), 134
Serman, Consul General Romain, 237
Shaw, Captain Jorge, 33
Shrivenham (England), 217
Siegel, Bugsy, 63
Sicily: invasion of, 86; Patton in, 96
Silver Star, 132, 167, 215, 228; for
Lothian, 187–88; for McGrew and
Lane, 186; for Orsbon, 139; and
Patton's hospital visit, 174–75
Singling (France), 158–59
65th Armored Field Artillery
Battalion, 43, 44–45
66th Field Artillery Battalion, 125,
142, 143, 168, 228
Slocum, Major LeCount, 12
"Sly-Feelers Society," 171, *236*
Smith, Lieutenant Ed, 189
Sovacool, Lieutenant Bill, 79; death
of, 213–14
Soviet Union visit (1935), 8
Stakonis, Sergeant Pete, 204–5, 207,
224
Stalin, Joseph, 8, 13, 203, 206
Stanford University studies, 10–14,
17, 25; and debate team, 13–14
*Stars and Stripes, The*, 146–47, 176
Stimson, Henry L., 20

**T**

Tactics classes, 28, 36
Taylor, Sergeant Bill, 195–96
10th Infantry Battalion, 125
35th Tank Battalion, 125
37th Tank Battalion, 56, 127, 148, 163
*Time* magazine, 146–47

Troyes (France), 134–38, 139, 154, 164; return to, 229
Truitt, Lieutenant Harry, 48, *235*
22nd Field Artillery Battalion, 168

**U**

Üdersdorf (Germany), 182–83
Ulio, Major General James A., 22, 23
United Nations, 203
U.S. Committee on Public Information, 5
Utah Beach (France), 110–11, 112, 191, 228

**V**

Vannes (France), 123, 126–27
VE Day, 147, 208–9
Vendôme (France), 134
Vienna (Austria), 8
Volkssturm, 182; attack on road to Bayreuth, 196–97, 205; gravesite and, 225–27
von Killinger, Baron Manfred, 9
von Rundstedt, Field Marshal Gerd, 161

**W**

Wagner, Richard, 199; villa of, 199–201
Waldenburg (Germany) forced labor camp, 198–99
Wallace, Colonel Neil, 142, 143, 228
Walsh, Annette, 77

Walsh, Lieutenant/Captain Bill, 48–49, 52, 74, 77, 113 215, *235*, *236;* at Commercy, 142; in Paris, 169, 170, 171; at Wood's wedding, 89–90
Walt, Lieutenant Don (and brothers), 27, *72*
Warsaw (Poland), 8
*Washington, SS*, 83
West, Art, 144
Wilcox, Captain Judson D., 47, 49
Wilhelm II, Kaiser, 5
Wilson, President Woodrow, 5
Wood, Lieutenant Billy, 186
Wood, Lieutenant Darrell, 88, *104*, *235;* wedding of, 89–90
Wood, George, 183
Wood, Major General John S. (Tiger Jack), 57, 95, 99, 110, 127, 147, 150, 228; removal of, from Fourth Armored, 159–60
World War I, xiv, 5, 6, 11, 42; howitzers in, 29; tunnels, 156
Wren friend. *See* Glew, Edna Frances

**X**

Xanrey (France), 156

**Y**

Yalta Conference, 203

**Z**

Zelinski, Sergeant Walter, 183

29932634R00163

Made in the USA
San Bernardino, CA
01 February 2016